Mystic Brews

Mystic Brews

A Seannchaidh's Guide to Story & Spirit

Mark S. C. McAlpin

Copyright

Published by ThistleStone

ISBN: 979-8-9945343-1-1
Printed by Lulu

This book is a work of nonfiction. All recipes, stories, and cultural references are presented for entertainment and educational purposes only. The author and publisher make no claims regarding the accuracy or efficacy of any historical or folkloric content.

First hardcover edition, 2026

9 798994 534311

For those who carried the stories before us.

Agus dhaibhsan a bheir iad air adhart.

The Calling of the Seannchaidh

Before the fire is lit, before the glass is raised,
before the first word finds its breath—
we pause.

We honor the land that shaped us,
the voices that carried us,
and the stories that refuse to fade.

Come forward now.
Step into the quiet between worlds.
Let the mist part.
Let the memory speak.

Author's Note

The earliest seed of this book arrived in the most ordinary way imaginable: a conversation with a friend about the old tale of the Mermaid's Curse. We weren't discussing folklore in any formal sense — just trading stories the way people do when the night runs long and the whisky runs warm. At one point, my friend laughed and said the name sounded like it belonged on a cocktail menu, not in a legend. That offhand remark stayed with me. It reminded me that stories live not only in archives and old books, but in the easy, passing exchanges between people. The Mermaid's Curse became, for me, a reminder that heritage is carried forward through these small, human moments as much as through any written record.

Preface

Long before this book had a structure or a name, it had a moment — a small one, almost forgettable. A friend was recounting the old tale of the Mermaid's Curse to us over drinks, speaking of it the way one speaks of weathered stories passed down through families and coastlines. We listened, smiled, and said the name would make a fine cocktail. The comment was lighthearted, but something in it struck me. It revealed how folklore slips easily between worlds: from the solemn to the playful, from the ancient to the modern, from the hearth to the barstool. That single exchange reminded me that these stories endure not because they are preserved, but because they are *carried* — reshaped, reimagined, and retold in every generation.

Moments like that reminded me that stories are not fixed artifacts; they are living companions, shaped by the land and carried forward by the people who hold them. And in the Highlands, that truth reveals itself everywhere you turn.

Every place carries a story. Every story carries a flavor.

And every flavor carries a memory.

The Highlands taught me that.

This book is not simply a collection of drinks—it is a map of moments, myths, and the people who shaped them. It is a way of remembering.

If you feel the land beneath these pages, then the work has done its job.

Acknowledgments

No book is ever written alone. It is shaped by the people who stand beside you, the ones who steady your hand, challenge your assumptions, and remind you why the work matters.

To my family, who carried me through the long hours and the quiet doubts — thank you for giving me the space to follow this thread of story and memory wherever it led. Your patience and encouragement made this book possible.

To my friends, especially the ones who listened to early fragments of folklore and half-formed ideas, thank you for the laughter, the questions, and the conversations that sparked entire chapters. One of those moments — a simple exchange about the Mermaid's Curse and how it sounded like a cocktail — became a turning point in this project. It reminded me that stories live not only in the past, but in the present, in the easy warmth of shared company.

To the Highlands themselves — the land, the weather, the silence, the stubborn beauty — thank you for teaching me that every place carries a story, and every story carries a flavor. This book is, in many ways, a love letter to that truth.

And finally, to every reader who opens these pages with curiosity and care: thank you for stepping into this world with me. May the stories and spirits within it meet you exactly where you are.

Introduction

This is a book about story and spirit—in every sense of the word.

It began with a simple question: what if a cocktail could carry a story? What if a drink could echo a legend, or hold the mood of a place the way a tale does? From that spark grew the recipes and rituals gathered here.

Think of this as a companion for evenings when the world slows down and the old stories rise—when a name like the Mermaid's Curse feels less like a drink and more like a doorway.

How To Use

This book is meant to be wandered through, not followed like a manual.

Each recipe carries three threads:

The Story — the myth, memory, or moment that shaped the drink.

The Craft — the ingredients, method, and sensory notes.

The Ritual — how to serve, share, or experience it.

You can begin with whichever thread calls to you.

Some readers start with the stories, letting the folklore lead them.

Others begin with the glass, tasting their way into the tale.

There is no wrong path.

Move through these pages the way you would walk a familiar glen—

slowly, curiously, letting the land and the stories guide your steps.

Content

THE STORY BEGINS

Before the first sip, there is the story. The Seannchaidh, the traditional Gaelic storyteller, opens the door to a world where myth and memory intertwine. These first two cocktails honor the oral tradition and the legends that echo through time.

CHAPTER 1

THE BEGINNING

"GUN TOIR AN SGEUL THU DHACHAIGH."
"MAY THE STORY BRING YOU HOME."

Before the first recipe is mixed or the first tale is poured, there is a moment of quiet — a breath where memory gathers itself. Every tradition begins this way: with someone willing to listen, and someone willing to speak. In the Highlands, that role belonged to the Seann-chaidh, the keeper of stories, who carried the weight of lineage in their voice and offered it freely to those gathered around the hearth.

This chapter opens the door to that ancient rhythm. It invites you to sit close, to let the world slow, and to feel the first threads of story take hold. What follows is not merely a cocktail, but a beginning — a way of stepping into the lineage of taste, tale, and tradition that this book traces.

The Seannchaidh

Ingredients:

- 1 oz gin
- 1/2 oz elderflower liqueur
- 1/2 oz blackberry liqueur
- 1/2 oz lemon juice
- 1/2 oz honey syrup
- A dash of Angostura bitters
- A dash of sparkling water
- Garnish: lemon twist and a sprig of rosemary for garnish

Directions

1. Fill a cocktail shaker with ice.
2. Add the gin, elderflower liquer, blackberry liquer, lemon juice and a dash of Angosture biters to the shaker.
3. Shakewell until the mixture is chilled.
4. Strain mixture into a glass filled with ice.
5. Top with a dash of sparking water.
6. **Garnish with a lemon and spring of rosemary.**

The Seannchaidh — pronounced shan-a-key — is the keeper of memory in the Gaelic world, a storyteller whose voice bridges the living and the long-departed. Their task was never merely to entertain. They carried the lineage of a people: the triumphs, the griefs, the migrations, the oaths, the quiet domestic moments that would otherwise vanish into the heathered wind. A Seannchaidh held these stories in trust, speaking them aloud so they remained alive, renewed each time they were told.

In the Highlands, stories were not recited as fixed artifacts. They were shaped in the moment — adapted to the listeners gathered around the hearth, the season, the weather, the needs of the clan. A good Seannchaidh could read a room as deftly as a piper reads a reel, adjusting cadence, emphasis, and silence until the tale settled into the bones of those who heard it.

This cocktail, The Legend, is crafted in that same spirit of living tradition. Its ingredients echo the Seannchaidh's role: the brightness of gin for clarity of voice, the floral sweetness of elderflower for memory preserved, the dark berry depth for the weight of old stories, and the lift of sparkling water for the breath that carries them forward. It is a drink meant not just to be tasted, but to be shared in company — because a story, like a good cocktail, is never complete until it is offered to someone else.

To raise this glass is to honor the ancient rhythm of telling and listening, of holding and releasing, of remembering and renewing. It is a small ritual of connection — a reminder that every family, every place, every name carries its own legends waiting to be spoken aloud.

The Legend

Ingredients:

- 1 1/3 oz   Vodka
- 1/3 oz   Blackberry Liqueur
- 2/3 oz   Lime Juice
- 2 Dashes   Orange Bitters
- 2/3 oz   Simple Syrup

Directions

1. Fill cocktail shaker with ice.
2. Add all the ingredients to the cocktail shaker
3. Shake vigorously
4. Strain into cocktail glass

Legends are the soul of a culture—stories passed from voice to voice, generation to generation, shaped by time but never forgotten. They are the whispered truths behind the wind on the moors, the flicker of light in the forest, the ripple across a still loch. In Scotland, legends are not just tales—they are living echoes of the land itself. From the heroic deeds of warriors to the mysterious enchantments of the fae, these stories form a tapestry of wonder, warning, and wisdom.

To sip The Legend is to drink in that legacy. This cocktail is a tribute to the timeless power of myth. The vodka, clear and strong, represents the enduring spirit of the Highland heroes—resilient, bold, and unyielding. The blackberry liqueur, dark and rich, evokes the brambles and shadows of ancient forests where secrets lie hidden. Lime juice and orange bitters bring a sharp, invigorating brightness, like the sudden twist in a tale or the chill of a Highland breeze. And the simple syrup? That's the storyteller's charm—a touch of sweetness that lingers long after the tale is told.

Raise your glass to the legends that shaped a nation. Let the flavors guide you through misty glens, over stormy seas, and into the heart of myth itself. With every sip, The Legend invites you to become part of the story.

In the pages that follow, you'll discover cocktails inspired by the myths, creatures, and heroes of Scotland's storied past. Each recipe is a tribute to the tales that shaped a nation—crafted to stir the imagination as much as the senses. Let The Legend be your first step into a world where every sip tells a story.

THE BEGINNING

Stories do not end so much as they settle — like the last swirl of color in a glass before it clears. With The Legend, you've taken your first step into a tradition shaped by memory, voice, and the quiet power of gathering. The Seannchaidh knew that every tale, no matter how small, carried the potential to bind people together.

As you move forward, let this first chapter be your anchor. Let it remind you that every recipe in these pages is more than a set of instructions. Each one is a fragment of heritage, a spark of place, a whisper of the past carried into the present. And like all good beginnings, it opens the way for what comes next.

THE BEGINNING

Windswept moors, ancient stones, and the howl of the Cu-Sith—these drinks are steeped in the wild, untamed spirit of the Highlands. Each recipe is a toast to the land of mist and myth. Inspired by myths and legends rooted in the Scottish Highlands.

CHAPTER 2

HIGHLAND ECHOES

"FAR AM BI GAOTH NA BEINNE, 'S ANN A CHLUINNEAR GUTH NAN SEANN SGEUL."

"WHERE THE MOUNTAIN WIND BLOWS, THE VOICES OF OLD STORIES ARE HEARD."

Where wind, stone, and story converge.

Across the windswept moors of the Highlands, where ancient stones stand like sentinels and the cry of the Cù-Sìth rides the dusk air, the land itself seems to breathe. Mist curls through the heather, peat smoke drifts from distant hearths, and every glen holds a memory older than any written tale. These cocktails are shaped by that wildness — steeped in the untamed spirit of the Highlands, where myth and landscape are inseparable.

Each recipe in this chapter is a toast to the rugged beauty of the north: the twilight hours when the veil thins, the winter storms ruled by the Cailleach, the spectral hounds that guard the moors, and the thistle-bright resilience of the clans who called this land home. Raise your glass to the echoes carried on Highland winds — for here, every sip is a story.

Highland's Twilight

A dusk-lit libation inspired by the gloaming of the Highlands.

Ingredients:

- 1 oz gin
- 1 oz elderflower liqueur
- 1 oz blueberry lavender simple syrup
- ½ oz tart cherry juice
- 1 oz ginger beer
- Ice
- Lavender sugar

Directions

1. Rim a martini glass with the lavender sugar
2. Shake gin, elderflower liqueur, lavender blueberry syrup and tart juice with ice.
3. Strain into a prepared chilled glass.

The name Highland's Twilight evokes that quiet, spellbound hour when the Highlands shift from gold to violet and the land seems to breathe in unison with the fading light. It is a moment long honored in Scottish tradition — a liminal threshold where day yields to night and the world softens at the edges. In folklore, this is the hour when the veil between realms thins, and the Sìth — the fae folk of the glens and moors — are said to stir from their hidden places. Travelers once paused at twilight, not out of fear, but out of reverence for a time when myth and reality walk side by side.

The Highland's Twilight cocktail is crafted to echo that sense of gentle enchantment. The gin forms a crisp, cooling foundation, like the first breath of evening air sweeping across the heathered hills. Elderflower liqueur adds a soft floral lift, reminiscent of heather blooming along the ridges, its fragrance carried on the breeze. The blueberry-lavender syrup deepens the drink to a twilight purple, mirroring the sky as it slips toward dusk, while the tart cherry juice introduces a subtle bittersweetness — the emotional undertone of so many Highland tales.

A final splash of ginger beer brings brightness and a hint of unpredictability, a nod to the lively, mercurial nature of the fae. Garnished with a sprig of lavender or a skewer of berries, the drink becomes a small ritual of its own — a toast to the hour when the Highlands glow with otherworldly color and the old stories feel close enough to touch.

Each sip invites you into that twilight space where memory, myth, and landscape intertwine, offering a taste of the Highlands at their most magical.

Highland Heather

A crimson-gold tribute to the moors, where heather blooms against the wind.

Ingredients:

- 1 1/2 oz Scotch whisky
- 1 oz cranberry juice
- 1/2 oz Drambuie
- 1/2 oz fresh lemon juice
- 1/2 oz honey syrup
- Ice
- Garnish: lemon twist and fresh cranberries

Directions

1. Fill a cocktail shaker with ice.
2. Add Scotch, cranberry juice, Drambuie, lemon juice, and honey syrup.
3. Shake well until chilled.
4. Strain into a rocks glass filled with ice.
5. Garnish with a lemon twist and fresh cranberries.

At the edge of twilight, when the last ember of daylight glows across the moors, the Highland Heather stirs to life. Cranberry juice spills into the glass like the rosy light of dawn, streaking across the amber depths of Scotch and Drambuie. A thread of honey syrup winds through the mixture, as if the nectar of heather blossoms has been coaxed into liquid form.

Centuries ago, clans gathered on heather-carpeted slopes to mark the midsummer solstice, weaving garlands of purple blooms and singing songs to honor the land's resilience. One tale tells of a shepherdess who vanished into a hidden bog while chasing her lost lamb. Guided only by the scent of heather honey, her father found her nestled unharmed among cranberry-red blossoms, as though the moor itself had cradled her. Each sip of this cocktail carries that same sense of rescue, relief, and the moor's quiet generosity.

The first taste greets you with the smoky warmth of Scotch — a steadfast hearth against the Highland chill. Cranberry juice follows with a tart gust, echoing the wind-swept ridges. Drambuie lends its herbal sweetness, heather honey distilled into legend, while lemon juice snaps like a sudden shaft of sunlight through mist. Honey syrup rounds the edges, leaving a lingering warmth as gentle and persistent as the stubborn heather that blooms even in the harshest terrain.

Garnished with a curl of lemon peel and cranberries bobbing like morning dew, the Highland Heather becomes a portrait of the Highlands in a glass. Each berry mirrors the scattered blooms across the moor, and the lemon twist curls like a bracken frond shivering in the breeze. Lift your glass and let the Highland Heather bloom on your tongue — a journey across wildflower-strewn hills, a taste of clan tradition, and a reminder that beauty often rises from rugged ground.

The Cailleach

A winter-forged libation honoring the Veiled One, shaper of storms and stone.

Ingredients:

- 2 oz Scotch whisky
- 1 oz Drambuie
- 1/2 oz fresh lemon juice
- 1/2 oz honey syrup
- 2 dashes Angostura bitters
- Garnish: lemon twist

Directions

1. Fill a shaker with ice.
2. Add the Scotch whisky, Drambuie, lemon juice, honey syrup, and Angostura bitters.
3. Shake well until chilled.
4. Strain into a chilled cocktail glass.
5. Garnish with a lemon twist.

In the oldest Highland tales, the Cailleach — the Veiled One — strides across the land as winter's sovereign. She is the ancient architect of mountains, the keeper of storms, the cold breath that sweeps across the moors. With her staff she shapes the earth, carving valleys and raising peaks, her presence marking the turning of the seasons and the onset of the dark half of the year.

Some stories cast her as a fearsome hag with blue skin and white hair, others as a wise guardian of animals and wild places. In many traditions she is dual-natured: a winter crone who transforms into a maiden at spring's first light, embodying the eternal cycle of death and renewal. Her myths remind the Highlands that beauty and harshness often share the same breath.

This cocktail mirrors her essence — powerful, elemental, and steeped in contrast. The Scotch whisky evokes the rugged landscape she shaped, its smoky depth echoing the windswept ridges and ancient stones. Drambuie adds warmth and complexity, a nod to her hidden wisdom and the honeyed herbs of her lore. Lemon juice brings a bright snap, reflecting her springtime transformation, while honey syrup softens the edges like sunlight breaking through winter cloud. Angostura bitters add a grounding note, the balance she maintains between storm and stillness.

Lift the glass and you taste the Cailleach's dominion — the cold, the warmth, the wildness, the wisdom. A drink forged in winter's shadow, yet carrying the promise of returning light.

Cailleach's Frostbite

A sharp, winter-bright draught touched by the Queen of Winter's breath.

Ingredients:

- 2 oz Scotch whisky
- 1 oz elderflower liqueur
- 1 oz fresh lime juice
- 1/2 oz honey syrup
- 1/4 oz absinthe
- A dash of lavender bitters
- Ice
- Garnish: lime wheel and a sprig of thyme

Directions

1. Fill a cocktail shaker with ice.
2. Add the Scotch whisky, elderflower liqueur, lime juice, honey syrup, absinthe, and lavender bitters.
3. Shake well until chilled.
4. Strain into a chilled cocktail glass.
5. Garnish with a lime wheel and a sprig of thyme.

In Highland lore, the Cailleach reigns as the Queen of Winter, a formidable deity whose icy breath shapes the land. With a sweep of her staff she summons blizzards, freezes lochs, and sculpts frost across the heather. Her presence is both feared and revered — a reminder that winter is not merely a season, but a force of will, a test of endurance, and a keeper of ancient rhythms.

She is the guardian of wild creatures, the architect of storms, and the silent watcher of the long, dark months. Her touch can bring frostbite to the unprepared, yet her rule also preserves the land, allowing seeds to sleep beneath the frozen earth until spring's return. In her duality lies her power: harshness and protection, destruction and renewal.

Cailleach's Frostbite captures the bite of her winter dominion.
The Scotch whisky provides a sturdy backbone — the warmth needed to withstand her storms. Elderflower liqueur adds a fleeting floral brightness, like the rare beauty found in a snow-covered glen. Lime juice brings a sharp, bracing chill, echoing the Cailleach's cutting winds, while honey syrup softens the edges with a whisper of returning light. Absinthe introduces a hint of danger, a green flicker of the unknown, and lavender bitters lend a delicate, frost-kissed aroma.

Garnished with thyme and lime, the drink becomes a ritual of winter itself — a toast to the season's stark beauty and the ancient goddess who commands it. Each sip is a reminder of the icy balance she maintains: the cold that tests, the cold that protects, and the cold that shapes the Highlands into legend.

Cailleach's Blessing

A winter-deep draught touched by storm, silence, and the quiet renewal beneath snow.

Ingredients:

- 2 oz cherry-infused blended Scotch
- 3/4 oz Drambuie
- 1/2 oz fresh lemon juice
- 1/2oz honey syrup
- 2 dashes Angostura bitters
- Ice cubes
- Garnish: lemon twist and cherry

Directions

1. Add cherry-infused Scotch, Drambuie, lemon juice, honey syrup, and bitters to a shaker filled with ice.
2. Shake well until chilled.
3. Strain into a chilled cocktail glass.
4. Garnish with a lemon twist and a cherry.

Among the oldest Highland myths, the Cailleach stands as a paradox — a bringer of winter's fury and a guardian of the land's long sleep. Known as Beira, Queen of Winter, she strides across the mountains with her staff, summoning storms, shaping peaks, and blanketing the earth in frost. Her reign stretches from Samhain to Beltane, the dark half of the year when the world rests beneath her icy mantle.

She is often depicted as a towering, veiled woman with blue skin and white hair, her presence both fearsome and awe-inspiring. Yet her power is not solely destructive. In many traditions, the Cailleach's winter is a necessary stillness — a time of preservation, reflection, and hidden renewal. Beneath her frost, seeds sleep. Beneath her storms, the land gathers strength. And at Imbolc, she transforms into the maiden Brigid, heralding the return of spring.

This cocktail honors that dual nature — the harshness and the blessing intertwined.

The cherry-infused Scotch brings a deep, ruby warmth, echoing the dark fruit of winter and the smoky breath of peat fires burning against the cold. Drambuie adds honeyed herbs, a whisper of ancient remedies and hearth-side lore. Lemon juice cuts through with a bright, awakening snap, while honey syrup softens the edges like the first thaw. Angostura bitters ground the drink with a hint of shadow — the memory of storms past.

Lift the glass and you taste the Cailleach's gift: not gentleness, but endurance; not comfort, but clarity; not warmth, but the promise of warmth returning. Her blessing is the reminder that even in the deepest winter, life waits beneath the snow, gathering strength for the season to come.

The Cu-Sith

*A deep-green draught echoing the silent paws and
spectral breath of the faerie hound.*

Ingredients:

- 2 oz Scotch
- 1 oz Green Chartreuse
- 1 oz Fresh lime juice
- 1/2 oz Honey syrup
- 2 dashes Angostura bitters
- 1 drop of green food coloring (optional)
- Ice cubes
- Garnish: fresh mint leaves

Directions

1. Add Scotch, Chartreuse, lime juice, honey syrup, bitters, and optional coloring to a shaker filled with ice.
2. Shake vigorously until well chilled.
3. Strain into a chilled cocktail glass.
4. Garnish with fresh mint.

Under the mist-laden moonlight of the Highlands, the Cù-Sìth prowls — a great faerie hound born of ancient magic and the wild breath of the moors. Its coat is said to shimmer a deep, unnatural green, as though woven from shadowed heather and the moss-dark earth. Silent as drifting fog, it moves through rocky clefts and hidden glens, a guardian spirit whose presence is felt long before it is seen.

By day, the Cù-Sìth remains unseen, slipping between worlds with the ease of a whispered tale. But at dusk, it unleashes three thunderous barks that echo across valleys and sea-washed cliffs. Legend warns that those who fail to seek shelter before the final bark may be claimed by the Otherworld, guided away by the hound's luminous eyes — green or red, depending on the tale — that pierce the veil between realms.

This cocktail captures the paradox of the Cù-Sìth: fierce yet protective, wild yet watchful. The Scotch whisky brings smoky warmth, the heartbeat of the Highlands. Green Chartreuse adds herbal depth, a whisper of faerie forests and hidden groves. Lime juice cuts through with a sharp, primal tang, while honey syrup softens the edges like a gentle breath in the cold night air. Angostura bitters add a faint bitterness, recalling the hound's grim reputation, and the optional green tint nods to its uncanny hue.

Mint leaves float atop the drink like leaves stirred by an unseen presence — a reminder of the hound's silent passage through the glens. Lift the glass and you can almost hear distant howls rolling over the hills, urging respect for the ancient pacts woven into the Highlands' heart.

The Cù Bòcan

A smoky-blue apparition in a glass, echoing the shifting form
of the Highland's ghost.

Ingredients:

- 2 oz peated Scotch whisky
- 1 oz Drambuie
- 1/2 oz fresh lemon juice
- 1/2 oz honey syrup
- 2 dashes Angostura bitters
- 1 drop of blue curaçao
- Ice cubes
- Garnish: lemon twist

Directions

1. Add Scotch, Drambuie, lemon juice, honey syrup, bitters, and optional curaçao to a shaker filled with ice.
2. Shake vigorously until well chilled.
3. Strain into a chilled coupe or rocks glass.
4. Garnish with a lemon twist.

Under the sapphire haze of twilight, the Cù Bòcan emerges — a spectral hound wreathed in drifting tendrils of blue smoke. Its form is said to shift like mist over the moors, revealing only a pair of glowing eyes that pierce the Highland gloom. Neither wholly benevolent nor malicious, the Cù Bòcan is an enigmatic sentinel, a creature of the in-between whose presence lingers long after it vanishes into the night.

The first breath of this cocktail mirrors that haunting arrival.
Peated Scotch whisky brings a fierce, smoky intensity — the cold, bracing air of a Highland glen captured in spirit. Drambuie softens the edges with honeyed herbs, a whisper of faerie lore woven into the drink's heart. Lemon juice cuts through with a bright, cleansing snap, while honey syrup rounds the flavors into a warm, lingering glow. A single drop of blue curaçao swirls into the amber depths, conjuring the hound's ghostly veil of smoke.

Legend tells of a distillery hand at Tomatin who once encountered the Cù Bòcan wandering the grounds at dusk. Drawn by curiosity, he reached out to touch its mist-shrouded pelt — and felt only the chill of something not quite of this world. In the next breath, the hound dissolved into thin air, leaving behind the faint scent of peat and the echo of a story that would outlive him.

This cocktail honors that moment of contact — the fleeting brush with the supernatural, the shimmer of something ancient slipping just beyond reach. As you cradle the glass, imagine the hound's luminous gaze, the hush that follows its passing, and the quiet promise that even in the darkest glens, a guardian may be watching from the shadows.

The Ginger

A winter-bright tempest of spice and sea, rising like a warm gale against the northern cold.

Ingredients:

- 2 oz rum
- 1/2 oz Amontillado sherry
- 1 oz fresh lime juice
- 1 oz gingerbread syrup
- 4 dashes Angostura bitters
- Miracle Foamer
- Garnish: spritz Paychaud's bitters

Directions

1. Dry shake all ingredients to build a rich foam.
2. Add ice and shake again until well chilled.
3. Strain into a chilled coupe glass.
4. Garnish with a light spritz of Peychaud's bitters across the foam.

When the north wind howls across the rum-dark sea, The Ginger rises in your glass like a cresting winter wave. Golden Caribbean rum forms the drink's warm, molasses-rich heart, while Amontillado sherry adds a dusky whisper of oak and dried fruit — the flavor of storm-weathered timbers and old ship hulls. Lime juice cuts through the dusk like a lantern swinging in a gale, and gingerbread syrup weaves its cozy warmth through every sip, echoing the scent of hearthfires burning against the cold.

Legend tells of a shipwreck off a frost-bitten island, where mariners clung to life as icy waves battered the shore. In the wreck's galley, they found a hidden cache of spices — ginger, clove, cinnamon — and a barrel of rum miraculously intact. With these, they brewed a warming draught whose foamy crown disguised the meager ingredients beneath. By morning, the survivors sang ballads of the gingered elixir that tasted of hope, hearthlight, and the promise of dawn.

This cocktail carries that same spirit of survival and solace.
Rum brings depth and warmth, the steadying heartbeat of the drink. Sherry adds a nutty duskiness, a nod to the old maritime routes that once ferried barrels across storm-tossed waters. Lime juice cracks open the sweetness with bright tension, while gingerbread syrup envelops the palate in notes of baked ginger, molasses, and brown sugar. Angostura bitters stitch in shadowy spice, and the foamy head — lifted by Miracle Foamer — mimics the crest of a winter wave.

A spritz of Peychaud's bitters drifts across the surface like a final breath of color against a snow-tipped shore. Raise this glass and you join the circle of wanderers warmed against the night, sharing a drink that tastes of resilience, memory, and the quiet fire that keeps the cold at bay.

Thistle Sour

A floral-bright Highland bloom, rising against rugged stone like Scotland's own emblem.

Ingredients:

- 2 oz Scotch whisky
- 3/4 oz Fresh lemon juice
- 1/2 oz Simple syrup
- 1/2 oz Crème de Violette
- Egg white (optional, for a frothy texture)
- Garnish: lemon twist and a violet flower

Directions

1. Dry shake Scotch, lemon juice, simple syrup, Crème de Violette and egg white.
2. Add ice and shake again until well chilled.
3. Strain into coupe glass
4. Garnish with a lemon and violet flower
5.

At the moment the sun dips behind the cragged Highland horizon, the Thistle Sour awakens — a delicate bloom set against rugged stone. Pouring Scotch whisky into the shaker summons the heather-haunted hills, while fresh lemon juice snaps like dawn's first light breaking across the moors. Simple syrup softens the edges, and crème de violette lends a pale lavender hue, as if you've captured the fleeting blush of a thistle in early spring.

Legend tells of a warrior king pursued by Norse raiders. Under cover of night, the invaders crept barefoot across a field — until one stepped upon a hidden thistle. His cry shattered the silence, alerting the king's guards and turning the tide of battle. In this cocktail, every sip recalls that moment of revelation: the bracing tang of lemon for alarm, the whisky's warmth for courage, and the syrup's sweetness for the mercy that followed.

Crème de violette unfolds like a faerie garden at twilight, its floral perfume weaving between the malted peat of the whisky. A frothy swirl of egg white — optional yet transformative — mimics the swirling Highland mists that cloak the glens before dawn. In those ephemeral wisps, you sense the gentle watch of ancient spirits, guardians of land and lore.

Garnished with a spiral of lemon peel and a single violet blossom, the Thistle Sour becomes a living emblem of Scotland's national flower. The citrus twist curls like a thistle's prickly leaves, while the violet nods to hidden beauty and resilience. Lift the glass and feel the melody of contrasts: bold whisky and soft florals, tart lemon and sweet syrup, solid spirit and ephemeral froth. A drink that honors the thistle's tenacity — blooming where few others dare.

Thistle's Charm

A bright, berry-kissed enchantment woven from Highland wit, wild fruit, and loch-side magic.

Ingredients:

- 1 1/3 oz vodka
- 1/3 oz blackberry liqueur
- 2/3 oz fresh lime juice
- 2/3 oz lavender-and-sea simple syrup
- 1 oz tart cherry juice
- 2 dashes orange bitters
- Garnish: none specified (optional: violet, blackberry, or citrus twist)

Directions

1. Fill a cocktail shaker with ice.
2. Add vodka, liqueur, cherry juice, lime juice, and simple syrup to the shaker.
3. Shake well until the mixture is chilled.
4. Strain the mixture into a martini glass
5.

Thistle's Charm whispers with the mischief and resilience of Scotland's national emblem. In Highland lore, the thistle is more than a flower — it is a guardian, a symbol of sharp wit and unexpected beauty, blooming defiantly where few others dare. This cocktail draws from that spirit, weaving together flavors that echo the land's rugged grace and its deep well of stories.

Vodka forms the drink's clear, steady backbone — the strength of Highland warriors who once stood against invaders on heathered slopes. Blackberry liqueur brings the dark sweetness of wild berries gathered in faerie-touched forests, where legends say the Sìth wander at dusk. Lime juice and orange bitters add a bright, cutting edge, reminiscent of the sharp humor of Robert Burns, whose verses could charm or sting with equal precision.

The lavender-and-sea simple syrup carries the quiet magic of the lochs — floral, saline, and serene — where selkies are said to slip from seal to human beneath the moon's silver gaze. Tart cherry juice deepens the drink with a crimson glow, recalling the blood-red sunsets that fall over the cliffs after ancient battles, when the air still hums with the echoes of pipes and the whispers of unseen spirits.

Lift the glass and you taste a spell of contrasts: wild fruit and bright citrus, floral calm and bracing bite, land and sea intertwined. Thistle's Charm is a toast to the Highlands' enduring magic — a drink that blooms boldly, beautifully, and with just a hint of enchantment.

Cherry Highland Fling

A smoky-crimson dance of fruit and fire, echoing the passion and poetry of Highland twilight.

Ingredients:

- 2 oz cherry-infused blended Scotch
- 1 oz sweet vermouth
- 1/2 oz cherry liqueur
- 1/2 oz fresh lemon juice
- 2 dashes Angostura bitters
- Ice
- Garnish: lemon twist and cherry

Directions

1. Add cherry-infused Scotch, sweet vermouth, cherry liqueur, lemon juice, and bitters to a shaker filled with ice.
2. Shake well until chilled.
3. Strain into a chilled cocktail glass.
4. Garnish with a lemon twist and a cherry.

In the heart of the Highlands, where heather blooms and lochs shimmer like polished glass, there is a tale whispered among the glens. It speaks of a lone cherry tree growing at the water's edge — a tree said to bloom only when two souls danced beneath it in perfect harmony.

One twilight during the Highland Games, a wandering bard and a spirited lass met beneath that very tree. As pipes keened across the hills and the sky blushed with dusk, they danced the Highland Fling with such fire that the cherry blossoms burst into bloom, showering them in crimson petals. Their kiss, legend says, tasted of smoke and fruit — a fleeting moment of joy that lingered like the last note of a reel drifting over the moor.

This cocktail captures the romance and rhythm of that enchanted dance.
Cherry-infused Scotch brings the smoky soul of the Highlands, its warmth echoing peat fires and the breath of evening winds. Sweet vermouth adds velvety depth, like the warmth of a lover's gaze across the firelight. Cherry liqueur infuses the drink with lush sweetness — the mythical tree's fruit distilled into spirit — while lemon juice adds a bright, tart twist, the thrill of the dance itself. Angostura bitters ground the drink in tradition, a nod to the old stories carried from hearth to hearth.

Lift the glass and you taste a dance in liquid form — bold, romantic, unforgettable. A toast to the lovers beneath the cherry tree, to the music that stirs the hills, and to the Highland nights where myth and memory entwine.

HIGHLAND ECHOES

In this chapter, the Highlands speak through wind, stone, and story. Each cocktail becomes a vessel for the land's ancient spirit, drawing from the twilight thresholds where the Sìth wander, the winter dominion of the Cailleach, and the spectral guardians who prowl the moors. The drinks move in a deliberate arc — from dusk's soft enchantment to the fierce breath of winter, from ghost-hound mysteries to the bright resilience of the thistle.

The chapter opens with the liminal glow of Highland's Twilight, where floral dusk and faerie lore intertwine. It deepens into the crimson warmth of Highland Heather, a tribute to wildflower-strewn moors and clan traditions. The heart of the chapter is shaped by the Cailleach — her storm-forged presence explored through three distinct cocktails that reflect her duality of destruction and renewal.

From there, the narrative slips into the Otherworld with the Cù-Sìth and Cù Bòcan, spectral hounds whose stories echo across peat-smoked glens. The chapter then turns toward maritime myth and winter spice with The Ginger, before blooming into floral resilience with the Thistle Sour and Thistle's Charm. It closes with the romantic legend of the Cherry Highland Fling, a dance of smoke, fruit, and twilight passion.

Together, these drinks form a tapestry of Highland myth — a journey through landscape, lore, and liminal light — inviting the reader to taste the stories carried on the wind.

From the selkies of the Hebrides to the monsters of the deep, the sea holds secrets and sorrow. These coastal concoctions capture the brine, beauty, and mystery of Scotland's waters.

CHAPTER 3

TALES OF THE SEA AND SHORE

"FAR AM BI TONN IS GAOTH, 'S ANN A DH'INNSEAS AN CUAN A SGEUL."

"WHERE WIND AND WAVE MEET, THE SEA TELLS ITS STORY."

Where tide and tale entwine, and every wave carries a whisper from the deep.

From the selkies of the Hebrides to the monsters that stir beneath black-water lochs, Scotland's coasts are shaped as much by story as by stone. Here, the sea is not merely a boundary but a living presence — a keeper of secrets, a giver and taker, a realm where the veil between worlds thins with every turning tide. Salt wind carries old songs across the surf, and the cries of seals echo like voices half-remembered from another life.

This chapter gathers cocktails inspired by those shoreline myths — drinks steeped in brine, beauty, and the haunting pull of the unknown. You'll meet selkie wives who shed their skins beneath moonlight, mermaids whose curses burn towns to ash, and water spirits who guard the depths with ancient patience. Each recipe is a small ritual, a way of tasting the stories that rise and fall with the tide.

Raise your glass to the sea's eternal rhythm — to the longing it awakens, the danger it conceals, and the mythic creatures who slip between its waves. For on these shores, every sip is a shoreline, every flavor a fragment of legend, and every cocktail a tale carried on the wind.

The Selkie Wife

A pale, moon-lit draught shaped by longing, loss, and the salt-soft pull of the tide.

Ingredients:

- 1 oz vodka
- 1 oz elderflower liqueur
- 1 oz white cranberry juice
- 1/2 oz fresh lemon juice
- A dash of sea salt
- Garnish: lemon twist

Directions

1. Add vodka, elderflower liqueur, white cranberry juice, lemon juice, and sea salt to a shaker filled with ice.
2. Shake well until chilled.
3. Strain into a chilled cocktail glass.
4. Garnish with a lemon twist.

On moon-washed shores where the tide breathes like a sleeping giant, selkies slip from their seal skins and dance upon the rocks. Their beauty is said to shimmer like wet silver, their laughter carried on the wind as softly as foam. Among these tales, none is more haunting than that of the Selkie Wife — a story of love bound by longing and undone by destiny.

A young fisherman once stumbled upon a circle of selkies dancing beneath the full moon. Entranced, he hid one maiden's seal skin, trapping her in human form. With no way to return to the sea, she became his wife, and together they built a life shaped by tenderness and quiet sorrow. Though she bore him children and tended their hearth, her gaze always drifted toward the horizon, where the waves whispered her true name.

Years later, it was their child — innocent and curious — who discovered the hidden skin. The selkie's heart surged with the pull of the deep. With a final, aching glance at the family she loved, she donned her seal form and slipped into the sea, leaving behind only the memory of her footsteps on the sand.

This cocktail captures that bittersweet tale — the brightness of love, the sting of loss, and the salt-touched longing that binds them.

Vodka brings clarity, like the cold northern waters where selkies rise. Elderflower liqueur adds a delicate floral sweetness, echoing the selkie's ethereal grace. White cranberry juice and lemon juice lend a pale, moonlit tartness — the sharp ache of a story that could never end gently. A pinch of sea salt ties the drink to the selkie's true home, the vast and restless sea. The lemon twist curls atop the glass like a final farewell.

Raise this glass and taste the Selkie Wife's journey — a love as fragile as foam, a longing as deep as the tide, and a story that lingers like salt on the wind.

The Selkie's Kiss

A bright, sea-spray spark of longing — the taste of a farewell sealed beneath moonlight.

Ingredients:

- 2 oz vodka
- 1 oz cranberry juice
- 1 oz fresh lime juice
- 1/2 oz simple syrup
- Club soda
- Ice
- Garnish : lime wedge and cranberries

Directions

1. Fill a cocktail shaker with ice.
2. Add vodka, cranberry juice, lime juice, and simple syrup.
3. Shake well until chilled.
4. Strain into a highball glass filled with ice.
5. Top with club soda and stir gently.
6. Garnish with a lime wedge and a few cranberries.

In the mist-soft coves of the northern isles, where the sea whispers secrets to the shore, selkies rise beneath the moon to shed their seal skins and walk the world of men. Their beauty is said to shimmer like wet pearl, their laughter drifting across the rocks like a song half-remembered from a dream.

One such tale tells of a fisherman who glimpsed a selkie dancing on the tide-slick stones. Drawn by her grace, he returned night after night, until she began to wait for him — a creature caught between two worlds, her heart tugged by the wild freedom of the sea and the fragile warmth of human love. Their meetings were fleeting, stolen moments beneath starlight, each one edged with the knowledge that dawn would break the spell.

On their final night, as the tide pulled hard toward the deep, she pressed a kiss to his lips — soft, bracing, and bittersweet. Then she slipped back into the waves, leaving behind only the memory of her touch and the salt-bright ache of a love that could never stay.

This cocktail captures that moment — the sting of parting, the brightness of desire, and the effervescence of something too wild to hold.

Vodka forms the clear, cold heart of the drink, like the northern waters where selkies rise. Cranberry juice adds a crimson glow, the color of passion and the sharp ache of goodbye. Lime juice cuts through with a bright, bracing snap — the kiss itself — while simple syrup softens the edges with a whisper of tenderness. Club soda lifts the drink with a gentle sparkle, like seafoam catching moonlight. Cranberries and lime drift atop the glass like offerings left on the tide.

Raise this glass and taste the Selkie's Kiss — fleeting, luminous, unforgettable.

The Selkie's Embrace

A dark-tide draught of smoke, brine, and moonlit longing — the moment a selkie steps from sea to shore.

Ingredients:

- 2 oz peated Scotch whisky
- 3/4 oz blackberry-brine syrup
- 1/2 oz fresh lemon juice
- 1/4 oz rich demerara syrup
- 2 dashes black walnut bitters
- Garnish: sea-salt foam, lemon twist and a blackberry "tide mark"

Directions

1. Fill a cocktail shaker with ice.
2. Add Scotch, blackberry-brine syrup, lemon juice, demerara syrup, and black walnut bitters.
3. Shake well until chilled.
4. Double-strain into a chilled cocktail glass.
5. Spoon a thin layer of sea-salt foam over the top to resemble a breaking wave.
6. Garnish with a lemon twist and a blackberry tide mark.

At the edge of the moon-silvered tide, where waves sigh against ancient stones, the Selkie's Embrace arrives like a memory half-remembered — or half-dreamed. In the hush between wave and wind, selkies shed their seal skins and rise in human form, their silhouettes shimmering like living water. Their presence is fleeting, their touch cool as sea-spray, their stories woven from longing and the pull of two worlds.

One tale tells of a sailor who found a selkie's discarded skin glinting on the rocks. Instead of hiding it, he returned it to her hands as the tide crept in. In that moment, she stepped close — eyes bright with gratitude, sorrow, and something deeper. She pressed her forehead to his, a gesture older than language, before slipping back into the surf. He never saw her again, but he swore the sea carried her warmth for years afterward.

Other stories speak of darker nights, when the sea turns glass-dark and the wind falls silent. A lone figure rises from the waves, hair slick with brine, eyes like storm light. She does not beckon. She simply waits. Those who step toward her are wrapped in arms cool and strong, and the sea folds over them like a closing door. Some return changed. Some do not return at all. But all who survive say the same thing: "It felt like drowning in a memory I didn't know I had."

This cocktail captures that haunting duality — the tenderness of a selkie's touch and the danger of the deep.

Peated Scotch brings smoky depth, like the shadowed waters where seals glide. Blackberry-brine syrup adds a dark, saline sweetness, echoing kelp forests and tide-pooled dusk. Lemon juice cuts through with a bright shaft of moonlight, while demerara syrup drifts in with soft warmth. Black walnut bitters deepen the drink with a whisper of ancient stone and storm-weathered cliffs. A crest of sea-salt foam mirrors the moment a selkie breaks the surface, and the blackberry tide mark recalls the line where sea meets shore — the boundary she can never fully cross.

Raise this glass and feel the Selkie's Embrace — cool, smoky, brined with longing, and gone too soon.

Selkie's Secret

A bright, tide-lit whisper of fruit and foam — a draught that tastes like something half-remembered from the deep.

Ingredients:
- 2 oz vodka
- 1 oz tart cherry juice
- 1 oz fresh lime juice
- 1/2 oz simple syrup
- Club soda
- Ice
- Garnish: lime wedge and cherries

Directions
1. Fill a cocktail shaker with ice.
2. Add vodka, cherry juice, lime juice, and simple syrup.
3. Shake well until chilled.
4. Strain the mixture into a highball glass filled with ice.
5. Top with club soda and stir gently.
6. Garnish with a lime wedge and a few cherries.

In the quiet stretch between sea and shore, where seals slip beneath moonlit waves and the air tastes faintly of salt and story, the selkies dwell. Neither wholly of the deep nor fully of the land, they move through the world like living secrets — creatures who shed their seal skins to walk among humans, leaving behind only wet footprints and the echo of a song carried on the tide.

Legends tell of selkies who fall in love, bear children, and vanish with the turning tide when their hidden skins are found. Others speak of selkies who keep their own counsel, visiting the shore only to watch, to listen, or to leave behind a single token — a smooth stone, a strand of kelp, a memory that feels like a dream. These are the selkie's secrets, the small mysteries that linger long after the waves erase their tracks.

This cocktail is a tribute to that liminal magic — the shimmer of something glimpsed and gone.

Vodka forms the drink's clear, still surface, like the calm of a hidden cove at dusk. Tart cherry juice brings a crimson glow, echoing the selkie's stolen passion and the bittersweet pull between freedom and love. Lime juice adds the sharp snap of sea wind, while simple syrup softens the edges with a whisper of warmth. Club soda lifts the drink with a gentle sparkle, like seafoam rising and falling with the tide.

Garnish it lightly — or not at all — for some secrets are best left unadorned.

Raise this glass and step into that threshold space where longing lingers, waves write stories no one fully knows, and the selkies keep their quiet watch beneath the moon.

The Mermaid's Curse

A sapphire-dark draught touched with sweetness, stormlight, and the sharp edge of a legend best left undisturbed.

Ingredients:

- 1/4 oz absinthe
- 1 oz blue curaçao
- 1 oz coconut rum
- 1 oz pineapple juice
- 1/2 oz fresh lime juice
- Garnish: edible glitter

Directions

1. Add absinthe, blue curaçao, coconut rum, pineapple juice, and lime juice to a shaker filled with ice.
2. Shake well until chilled.
3. Strain into a chilled cocktail glass.
4. Garnish with a light sprinkle of edible glitter to evoke the mermaid's enchanting allure.

Some tales of the sea arrive like soft tides; others crash ashore like a curse. The legend of The Mermaid's Curse belongs to the latter — a story of beauty wronged and magic unbound. In one telling, fishermen drag a mermaid from the water, dazzled by the shimmer of her scales and the strange music in her voice. Paraded through the town as a marvel, she gasps for breath as her skin dries in the air that is not her own.

With the last strength left in her drowning lungs, she speaks a curse — not in rage, but in something colder. Where her tears fall, flames will one day rise. Where her laughter is mocked, stone will crack and timber burn. Years later, when fire licks through hall and house, some swear they hear a distant, delighted laughter carried on the smoke.

This cocktail captures that seductive surface and darker undertow — a drink as dazzling as the mermaid herself, with an edge that hints she is not to be trifled with.

Absinthe forms the drink's otherworldly spine, its herbal bite like a flash of inhuman eyes beneath the waves. Blue curaçao paints the glass in oceanic sapphire, the color of deep water hiding old secrets. Coconut rum brings lush, tropical warmth — the intoxicating allure that draws sailors too close to the rocks. Pineapple juice adds sun-bright sweetness, while lime juice slices through with a tang that recalls the sting of salt and the sharpness of a spoken curse.

The final dusting of edible glitter scatters across the surface like scales catching light or embers caught in a sea wind — beautiful, dangerous, and unforgettable.

Lift this glass and remember: some enchantments are kind, some are cruel, and some — like the Mermaid's Curse — smile as they pull you under.

The Mermaid Bride

A sapphire-dark draught touched with sweetness, stormlight,
and the sharp edge of a legend best left undisturbed.

Ingredients:

- 1 oz vodka
- 1 oz blue curaçao
- 1 oz coconut cream
- 1/2 oz lime juice
- A dash of sparkling water
- A lime wheel for garnish

Directions

1. Combine vodka, blue curaçao, coconut cream, and lime juice in a shaker with ice.
2. Shake well and strain into a glass.
3. Top with a dash of sparkling water and garnish with a lime wheel

Along the rugged coasts where kelp forests sway like underwater cathedrals, the tale of the Mermaid Bride is whispered in the hush between waves. It is a story of love found, love held, and love surrendered — a reminder that the sea gives nothing without asking something in return.

One evening, a fisherman walking the tide line glimpsed a woman seated upon a rock, combing her hair with a shell that shimmered like moonlit glass. Only when she turned did he see the truth: she was a mermaid, her seal skin folded beside her like a discarded cloak. Entranced, he hid the skin, believing that without it she would remain with him. And so she did — not by choice, but by the strange, sorrow-soft magic that binds sea-folk to the land when their skins are taken.

They married. They raised children. Their home filled with laughter, warmth, and the scent of salt carried in on her hair. Yet she often stood at the window, gazing toward the horizon where the sea breathed in long, patient rhythms. Her smile was gentle, but her eyes held the ache of tides she could no longer follow.

One day, while playing, their child discovered the hidden skin. The mermaid's breath caught — not in joy, but in recognition. She kissed her family with a tenderness that broke the heart, then wrapped herself in her true form and slipped into the waves. Some say she looked back once. Others say she did not. But all agree that the sea welcomed her like a long-lost daughter.

This cocktail captures the bittersweet beauty of that tale — the warmth of love, the pull of the deep, and the shimmering moment where two worlds touch but cannot stay joined.

Vodka brings clarity, like the still surface of a calm sea. Blue curaçao paints the drink in oceanic sapphire, echoing the depths where mermaids dwell. Coconut cream adds lush, velvety warmth — the tenderness of the life she built on land. Lime juice cuts through with a bright, bracing tang, the sharp truth of her longing. A dash of sparkling water lifts the drink with a whisper of magic, like sunlight dancing on waves.

The lime wheel rests atop the glass like a small, bright moon — the same moon under which she first came ashore, and the one that watched her return to the sea.

Raise this glass to the Mermaid Bride — a story of love given freely, lost gently, and re-membered always.

The Seal Hunter

A dark-amber draught shaped by sorrow, sweetness,
and the sharp edge of choice that cannot be undone.

Ingredients:

- 1 oz dark rum
- 1 oz amaretto
- 1 oz pear juice
- 1/2 oz fresh lemon juice
- A dash of bitters
- Garnish: pear slice for garnish

Directions

1. Combine dark rum, amaretto, pear juice, lemon juice, and bitters in a shaker filled with ice.
2. Shake well until chilled.
3. Strain into a chilled cocktail glass.
4. Garnish with a pear slice.

Along the storm-bitten coasts where waves hammer the cliffs like ancient drums, the tale of the Seal Hunter is told in low voices — not as a warning, but as a lament. It is a story of desire, possession, and the terrible cost of holding what was never meant to be kept.

In the old days, seal hunters roamed the shores seeking pelts, meat, and oil. But some sought something rarer: the selkies themselves. For it was said that if a man stole a selkie's seal skin, she would be bound to him — unable to return to the sea, unable to reclaim her true form. Many a tale begins with a hunter who finds a selkie maiden dancing on the rocks, her skin folded beside her like a cloak of moonlit silver. Entranced, he hides it. And so she becomes his wife.

They build a life together — children, hearth, laughter — yet beneath it all lies a quiet ache. The selkie smiles, but her eyes drift always toward the horizon, where the tide breathes with her true heartbeat. She tends the home, loves her children, and moves through the world with a gentleness that breaks the heart. But she is never free.

One day, as in all such stories, her hidden skin is found — by a child, by chance, by fate. The selkie's breath catches. She touches her children's faces one last time, tears mingling with salt. Then she wraps herself in her true form and slips into the sea. Some say she looks back. Others say she does not. But all agree that the hunter stands alone on the shore, the waves washing over his footprints as if to erase the story entirely.

This cocktail captures the bittersweet duality of that tale — the warmth of love, the sweetness of memory, and the sharp sting of loss.

Dark rum brings depth and shadow, like the ocean at dusk. Amaretto adds a soft, almond sweetness — the tenderness of the life they shared. Pear juice lends delicate brightness, echoing the selkie's ethereal beauty. Lemon juice cuts through with a bracing tang, the truth he tried to hide. A dash of bitters grounds the drink in complexity, the emotional weight of a story that ends as it must.

The pear slice rests atop the glass like a small offering — a reminder of what was held, what was lost, and what was never his to keep.

Raise this glass to the Seal Hunter — a tale of love, longing, and the sea's quiet insistence on reclaiming its own.

Nessie's Elixir

A shimmering, sapphire draught of myth and mischief — bright as dawn on the loch, deep as the secrets beneath.

Ingredients:

- 2 oz gin
- 1 oz blue curaçao
- 1 oz fresh lemon juice
- 1/2 oz honey syrup
- A splash of tonic water
- Garnish: lemon twist and mint sprig

Directions

1. Fill a shaker with ice and add gin, blue curaçao, lemon juice, and honey syrup.
2. Shake well until chilled.
3. Strain into a highball glass filled with ice.
4. Top with a splash of tonic water.
5. Garnish with a lemon twist and a sprig of mint.

Beneath the mirrored surface of Loch Ness, wrapped in centuries of mist and rumor, dwells the most elusive spirit of all — the creature known simply as Nessie. Some call her a monster. Others call her a guardian. But those who know the loch best say she is something older, wiser, and far more mysterious than either word suggests.

Legends whisper that Nessie glides through the deep like a shadow of ancient time, surfacing only for those who believe without proof — those who listen to folklore not with their ears, but with their imagination. Fishermen speak of ripples that appear on windless days, of shapes glimpsed beneath the water like moving stone, of a presence that feels curious rather than cruel.

One tale tells of a traveler who camped on the loch's edge during a night so still the stars reflected perfectly on the water. As he dozed, he heard a soft splash — not threatening, but deliberate. When he looked up, he saw two luminous eyes watching him from the surface. Not hostile. Not afraid. Simply… aware. By morning, the only sign she had been there was a single ripple drifting toward shore, as if carrying a message he could almost understand.

This cocktail is a tribute to that sense of wonder — the shimmer of possibility, the thrill of the unknown, and the quiet magic that lingers where myth and water meet.

Gin forms the crisp, herbaceous backbone, like the cool breath of Highland air at dawn. Blue curaçao plunges the drink into a sapphire glow, echoing the loch's mysterious depths. Lemon juice adds a bright, searching light — the thrill of spotting something half-seen beneath the surface. Honey syrup smooths the blend with warmth, like folklore passed gently from voice to voice. A splash of tonic water adds sparkle, the ripple of excitement when myth stirs beneath fact.

The lemon twist curls like a glint of sunlight on water, and the mint sprig rises like a small green reed at the loch's edge.

Raise this glass to Nessie — to mystery without menace, to wonder without proof, and to the stories that surface only when the world grows quiet enough to hear them.

The Well at World's End

A bright, quest-born draught of citrus and courage — a sip shaped by trials, transformation, and the wisdom found at the edge of all things.

Ingredients:

- 2 oz tequila
- 1 oz grapefruit juice
- 1/2 oz lime juice
- 1/2 oz agave syrup
- Ice
- Garnish: grapefruit slice

Directions

1. Shake tequila, grapefruit juice, lime juice, and agave syrup with ice.
2. Strain into a glass filled with ice.
3. Garnish with a grapefruit slice.

In the old tales of Scotland, there is a place whispered about in the hush between hearth-fire stories — the Well at World's End, a spring said to lie at the farthest edge of the mortal realm. Those who seek it do so not for glory, but for transformation, for the well's waters are said to reveal one's true nature and grant the strength needed to face impossible trials.

One story tells of a young girl mistreated by her stepmother and sent on an impossible quest: fetch water from the Well at World's End using a sieve. The task was meant to break her spirit. But along her journey, she met a wise old woman who taught her to seal the sieve with moss and clay. With this simple act of ingenuity, the girl succeeded where she was meant to fail.

Her trials did not end there. She later encountered a magical frog whose strange demands tested her patience and kindness. When she met them with grace, the frog transformed into a prince — a reminder that compassion often reveals truths hidden beneath rough or unlikely forms.

This cocktail captures the resilience, clarity, and quiet triumph of that tale — a drink for those who have walked long roads, faced unfair burdens, and found their own way through.

Tequila brings strength and fire, the courage needed to begin any quest. Grapefruit juice adds a bright, bracing bitterness — the sting of hardship and the sharpness of truth. Lime juice cuts through with clarity, like the moment the girl realizes she can outwit the impossible. Agave syrup softens the blend with a whisper of sweetness, the reward earned through perseverance and kindness.

The grapefruit slice rests atop the glass like a rising sun — the promise that even at the world's end, renewal waits.

The Well of Youth

A verdant, light-struck draught of renewal — crisp as spring water, bright as a second chance, and touched with the quiet magic of rebirth.

Ingredients:

- 1 oz gin
- 1 oz elderflower liqueur
- 1 oz green tea syrup
- 1/2 oz lemon juice
- Garnish: cucumber slice

Directions

1. Combine gin, elderflower liqueur, green tea syrup, and lemon juice in a shaker filled with ice.
2. Shake well until chilled.
3. Strain into a chilled cocktail glass.
4. Garnish with a cucumber slice.

In the green-shadowed glens of Scotland, where moss grows thick as velvet and the air hums with the memory of old magic, stories whisper of a hidden spring known as the Well of Youth. Its waters are said to shimmer with a faint, unearthly glow — a light that does not come from sun or moon, but from the well's own ancient power.

According to legend, those who drink from the well feel their strength return, their spirits lift, and their hearts grow light as if touched by spring itself. But the well is not easily found. It lies beyond tangled forests and winding paths, guarded by creatures of leaf and shadow who test the worthiness of any traveler who seeks it. Only those who approach with humility, patience, and a true desire for renewal are granted passage.

One tale tells of a weary wanderer who stumbled upon the well after a long and difficult journey. Parched and near collapse, he cupped his hands and drank deeply. In an instant, warmth surged through him — not the heat of fire, but the gentle radiance of life return-ing. His limbs grew strong, his breath steady, and his eyes bright with the clarity of youth restored. When he looked into the water, he saw not the man he had been, but the man he could become.

This cocktail captures that freshness, vitality, and quiet transformation — a drink that tastes like the first green day of spring after a long winter.

Gin brings crisp botanical brightness, like the cool air around the well's hidden glade. Elderflower liqueur adds a delicate floral sweetness, echoing blossoms that bloom where magic lingers. Green tea syrup lends gentle herbal depth, the calm wisdom of ancient waters. Lemon juice cuts through with a clean, invigorating spark — the moment youth returns in a single breath.

The cucumber slice rests atop the glass like a leaf floating on still water — simple, pure, and alive.

Raise this glass to the Well of Youth — to renewal found in unexpected places, to journeys that restore us, and to the quiet magic that waits for those who seek it with an open heart.

TALES OF THE SEA AND SHORE

From selkies who slip between worlds to mermaids whose songs carry both wonder and warning, these shoreline stories remind us that the sea is never just water. It is memory. It is longing. It is the boundary where the known world ends and the mythic deep begins. Every cocktail in this chapter carries a fragment of that liminal magic — a taste of brine, a shimmer of moonlight, a whisper of something ancient rising beneath the waves.

The coast has always been a place of thresholds. Stand long enough at the water's edge and you feel it: the pull of tides older than language, the hush of stories carried on salt wind, the sense that something just beyond sight is watching with patient, curious eyes. These drinks invite you into that space — the shoreline between truth and tale, where each sip becomes a small ritual of remembrance.

As we leave the sea behind and turn inland once more, the echoes of these legends follow like the retreating tide. Their lessons linger: that freedom is precious, that love can be both anchor and storm, and that some mysteries are meant not to be solved, but savored.

Ahead lies a new landscape, shaped not by waves but by wind, stone, and shadow — a place where the land itself holds its own secrets, and where the next chapter waits with its own stories to tell.

TALES OF THE SEA AND SHORE

Step lightly—this is fae territory. These cocktails are inspired by the mischievous, magical, and mysterious beings that dwell in glens, groves, and twilight shadows.

CHAPTER 4
FAERIE REALMS AND
ENCHANTED WOODS

"ANNS NA COILLTEAN DORCHA, THA AN SAOGHAL EILE FAISG."

"IN THE DARK WOODS, THE OTHERWORLD IS NEAR."

Where twilight gathers beneath ancient boughs, and every path leads deeper into wonder.

Step softly here.
The forest is older than memory, and the faerie realms that lie within it are older still. In these green-shadowed places, the air hums with unseen wings, moss glows faintly under moonlight, and the boundary between mortal and otherworld grows thin as a whisper. Stories say the fae walk these woods at dusk, their footsteps light as falling petals, their laughter drifting through the trees like wind-chimes made of silver.

This chapter gathers cocktails shaped by those enchanted woods — drinks inspired by green spirits, twilight creatures, and the shimmering glamour that lingers where sunlight fades into shadow. Here you'll meet brownies who guard the hearth, glaistigs who haunt the glens, green women who tend the ancient groves, and tricksters who lead wanderers astray with a single flicker of light.

Each recipe is a small enchantment — a sip that tastes of leaf and loam, of moonlit paths and hidden doors, of the quiet magic that waits beneath every branch.

Raise your glass and step into the forest.
The fae are watching.

The Fairy Lover

A shimmering, herb-kissed draught of longing and enchantment — the taste of a love that crosses realms and cannot remain.

Ingredients:

- 1 oz absinthe
- 1 oz elderflower liqueur
- 1 oz pear juice
- 1/2 oz fresh lemon juice
- A dash of sparkling water
- Garnish: pear slice

Directions

1. Add absinthe, elderflower liqueur, pear juice, and lemon juice to a shaker filled with ice.
2. Shake well until chilled.
3. Strain into a chilled glass.
4. Top with a dash of sparkling water.
5. Garnish with a pear slice.

In the quiet glens where twilight pools like silver water, there are tales of mortals who fall in love with the fae — stories as beautiful as they are perilous. The Fairy Lover is one such tale, whispered in places where the veil between worlds grows thin and the air hums with unseen wings.

It begins with a young man wandering through a secluded glen at dusk. There, among the moss-soft stones, he sees her: a fairy maiden, radiant as moonlight on still water. Her beauty is not mortal beauty — it is sharper, brighter, edged with something ancient. He is entranced. Despite warnings from kin and clan, he returns night after night, drawn by her laughter, her grace, the way the air seems to shimmer around her.

Their love is fierce, intoxicating, and doomed. For the fairy realm follows its own laws, and mortals who linger too long in its shadow risk losing themselves. Some versions say he is taken away, vanishing into the otherworld with no path home. Others say she disappears at dawn, leaving him forever changed — touched by wonder, marked by longing.

This cocktail captures that bittersweet enchantment — the beauty of the encounter, the danger beneath it, and the lingering ache of a love that cannot stay.

Absinthe forms the drink's mystical backbone, its herbaceous bite echoing the sharp, intoxicating allure of the fae. Elderflower liqueur adds a delicate floral shimmer, the softness of her touch. Pear juice brings gentle sweetness, the purity of his devotion. Lemon juice cuts through with a bright sting — the truth that their worlds cannot remain entwined. A dash of sparkling water lifts the drink with a fleeting sparkle, like the moment she appears in the glen.

The pear slice rests atop the glass like a token left behind — a reminder of a love that was real, if only for a moment.

Raise this glass to the Fairy Lover — to beauty that dazzles, to longing that lingers, and to the stories that slip between worlds.

Faerie Glen Delight

A golden-twilight draught of orchard sweetness and quiet enchantment — a sip shaped by the soft magic of hidden glens and the laughter of unseen folk.

Ingredients:

- 2 oz vanilla vodka
- 2 oz apple cider
- 1/2 oz fresh lemon juice
- 1 tbsp caramel topping
- Cinnamon sugar (for rim)
- Garnish: apple slice

Directions

1. Rim a martini glass with caramel.
2. Dip the rim into cinnamon sugar.
3. Add vanilla vodka, apple cider, and lemon juice to a shaker filled with ice.
4. Shake well until chilled.
5. Strain into the prepared glass.
6. Garnish with an apple slice.

In the Highlands, tucked between moss-soft ridges and curling green knolls, lies a place whispered about in low, reverent tones: the Faerie Glen. It is a landscape that looks sculpted by whimsy — spirals of earth, miniature valleys, and strange, rounded hills that seem almost too deliberate to be natural. Locals say the glen is a place where the veil thins, where the fae dance in moonlit circles, and where time itself moves with a different rhythm.

Travelers who wander there speak of odd sensations:
the feeling of being watched by something gentle but curious,
the sound of distant bells with no visible source,
the flicker of light where no sunbeam falls.

Some claim that if you stand perfectly still at dusk, you may hear the faint hum of faerie music, drifting like wind through reeds.

This cocktail captures the warm, playful magic of that place — the sweetness of orchard fruit, the glow of autumn light, and the soft mischief that lingers in the air.

Vanilla vodka brings smooth warmth, like a faerie's laugh tucked into the folds of twilight. Apple cider adds crisp, golden sweetness — the taste of trees that grow in places no mortal hand has planted. Lemon juice cuts through with a bright spark, the sharp logic of the fae: unexpected, precise, and strangely perfect. Caramel swirls through the drink like a charm, thick with memory and the sweetness of harvest. The cinnamon-sugar rim adds the scent of wind-carried magic, and the apple slice gleams like a wing catching the last light of day.

To drink Faerie Glen Delight is to wander briefly into a world where stories grow wild, where the land itself seems to breathe, and where every sip feels like a small enchantment.

Taming the Kelpie

A deep-blue, storm-bright draught of danger and mastery — the taste of a creature born of dark waters and the courage required to claim its bridle.

Ingredients:

- 2 oz Scotch whisky
- 1 oz blue curaçao
- 1 oz fresh lemon juice
- 1/2 oz honey syrup
- 2 dashes Angostura bitters
- Ice
- Garnish: lemon twist and mint sprig

Directions

1. Add Scotch whisky, blue curaçao, lemon juice, honey syrup, and bitters to a shaker filled with ice.
2. Shake well until chilled.
3. Strain into a chilled glass filled with ice.
4. Garnish with a lemon twist and a sprig of mint.

In the deep lochs and swift rivers of Scotland, where mist clings to the water like breath on glass, there dwells a creature feared and revered in equal measure: the Kelpie. A shape-shifting water spirit, it most often appears as a magnificent black horse, its mane dripping like riverweed, its eyes bright with unnatural intelligence. But its beauty is a trap. Those who climb upon its back find themselves bound fast, unable to dismount as the Kelpie plunges into the depths, dragging its rider to a watery grave.

Yet the old stories also speak of rare mortals who managed the impossible — who seized the Kelpie's bridle and bent the creature to their will. To tame a Kelpie is to master fear itself, to claim dominion over the unknown, to hold the reins of something wild enough to drown the unwary and powerful enough to reshape fate.

This cocktail captures that tension between danger and triumph — the dark pull of the loch, the flash of courage, the moment the bridle is seized.

Scotch whisky forms the drink's rugged backbone, echoing the Kelpie's strength and the stony Highlands where such legends were born. Blue curaçao plunges the glass into the color of deep, enchanted water — beautiful, deceptive, and cold. Lemon juice slices through with sharp clarity, the moment of decision when fear becomes action. Honey syrup softens the edges, the sweetness of victory earned through peril. Bitters add depth and shadow, the reminder that even tamed, a Kelpie is never truly safe.

The lemon twist curls like a captured bridle, and the mint sprig rises like river reeds stirred by something powerful beneath the surface.

Raise this glass to the Kelpie — to the courage it demands, the danger it embodies, and the rare, fierce triumph of mastering what was meant to master you.

The Battle of the Birds

A bright, jewel-toned draught of conflict and cunning — a sip shaped by enchanted quests, shifting alliances, and the fierce beauty of winged magic.

Ingredients:

- 1 oz bourbon
- 1 oz apricot brandy
- 1 oz orange juice
- 1/2 oz grenadine
- Garnish: orange twist

Directions

1. Combine bourbon, apricot brandy, orange juice, and grenadine in a shaker with ice.
2. Shake well and strain into a glass filled with ice.
3. Garnish with an orange twist

Among Scotland's oldest and most intricate wonder tales, The Battle of the Birds stands apart — a story woven from riddles, enchantments, shapeshifting, and the strange alliances that form when fate twists its threads. It begins with a young prince who encounters a magical bird while hunting. But the bird is no mere creature of feather and bone — it is a king in disguise, bound by a curse and seeking a mortal brave enough to follow him into the otherworld.

The prince's journey leads him into a realm where nothing is as it seems. Birds speak in riddles. Giants guard impossible treasures. A princess waits in a tower of spells, her fate tied to the prince's courage. Every step forward requires wit, loyalty, and a willingness to trust creatures whose motives shimmer like heat-haze.

The "battle" itself is not merely a clash of wings — it is a metaphor for the clan feuds, shifting loyalties, and hidden politics that shaped Scotland's past. Each bird represents a lineage, a history, a rivalry. The prince must navigate these tensions with care, for one wrong choice could unravel the fragile alliances that keep him alive.

This cocktail captures the vibrant, perilous beauty of that tale — the flash of feathers, the heat of conflict, the sweetness of unexpected allies.

Bourbon forms the drink's bold foundation, the strength and resilience of the prince himself. Apricot brandy adds lush sweetness, the allure of the magical bird and the princess he seeks to save. Orange juice brings brightness and vitality, the spark of adventure that propels the tale forward. Grenadine deepens the color to a rich, battle-red hue — a reminder of the dangers faced and the blood that might be spilled. The orange twist curls atop the glass like a feather caught mid-flight, a final nod to the story's winged heart.

Raise this glass to the Battle of the Birds — to quests that test the spirit, to alliances forged in strange places, and to the bright, fierce beauty of stories that refuse to be forgotten.

The Tale of the Hoodie

A dark-fruited, shape-shifting draught — rich, sharp, and mysterious, like the crow-prince who walks between feather and flesh.

Ingredients:

- 1 oz dark rum
- 1 oz blackcurrant liqueur
- 1 oz fresh lime juice
- 1/2 oz simple syrup
- A dash of bitters
- Garnish: lime wheel

Directions

1. Add dark rum, blackcurrant liqueur, lime juice, simple syrup, and bitters to a shaker filled with ice.
2. Shake well until chilled.
3. Strain into a glass.
4. Garnish with a lime wheel.

In the old stories of Scotland, the Hoodie Crow is no ordinary bird. With feathers black as peat-smoke and eyes bright with cunning, it moves through the world with a knowing intelligence that hints at something more than animal instinct. And in one of the most enchanting tales, the Hoodie is revealed to be a prince — cursed, transformed, and bound to wander the wilds in feathered form until love and courage break the spell.

The tale begins with a young woman who encounters the Hoodie in the forest. He speaks to her — not in the caw of a crow, but in the voice of a man hidden beneath the glamour. He asks for her help, for only kindness freely given can unravel the enchantment that binds him. Their journey together is filled with trials: giants with iron clubs, witches who weave fate like thread, and riddles that twist like smoke. Through it all, the Hoodie shifts between forms, neither fully bird nor fully man, caught in the liminal space where magic clings like mist.

This cocktail captures the mystery, transformation, and dark allure of that tale — the sharp wit of the crow, the hidden warmth of the prince, and the strange beauty of a love forged in the shadowed glens.

Dark rum forms the drink's deep, brooding base — the weight of the curse and the strength of the prince beneath it. Blackcurrant liqueur adds a dark, jewel-toned sweetness, the richness of enchantment and the pull of the unknown. Lime juice slices through with bright, unpredictable energy, the sudden turns and clever escapes that define the Hoodie's journey. Simple syrup softens the edges, the moments of tenderness that reveal the prince's true heart. A dash of bitters adds complexity, the trials that shape him. The lime wheel rests atop the glass like a turning wheel of fate — ever shifting, ever circling back.

Raise this glass to the Hoodie — to transformation, to cleverness, and to the strange, beautiful paths that lead us toward our truest selves.

The Maker of Dreams

A lavender-lit draught of mystery and moonlight — a sip shaped by the quiet alchemy of sleep, story, and the ancient hands that craft the visions of the night.

Ingredients:

- 1 oz vodka
- 1 oz lavender syrup
- 1 oz fresh lemon juice
- 1/2 oz crème de violette
- A dash of club soda
- Garnish: lavender sprig

Directions

1. Add vodka, lavender syrup, lemon juice, and crème de violette to a shaker filled with ice.
2. Shake well until chilled.
3. Strain into a chilled glass.
4. Top with a dash of club soda.
5. Garnish with a lavender sprig.

On the Isle of Skye, where mist drifts like wandering spirits and the Black Cuillin rise like the bones of ancient giants, there is a tale whispered only in the soft hours before dawn — the story of the Makers of Dreams. It begins with a young girl lost in a fog thick enough to swallow the world. Guided by a silent herd of deer, she finds herself at the mouth of a hidden cave, a place untouched by time.

Inside, she meets an elderly couple — ageless, gentle, and strange. They are the Makers of Dreams, the quiet artisans who shape the visions that visit sleeping minds. By lamplight, they mold dreams from curds of cheese, pressing them into forms both beautiful and terrible. Birds carry these creations into the night, delivering them to children and wanderers alike. Some dreams soothe. Others warn. All of them teach.

The tale reminds us that dreams are not accidents — they are messages, mirrors, and mysteries, shaped by forces older than memory.

This cocktail captures the soft magic and twilight wonder of that story — the hush of the cave, the glow of the lamplight, the delicate balance between comfort and revelation.

Vodka brings clarity, the clean brightness of the dream-world before form takes hold. Lavender syrup adds soothing floral sweetness, the calm that settles over the mind as sleep begins. Lemon juice cuts through with sharp insight, the sudden clarity a dream can bring. Crème de violette deepens the drink with a violet-hued mystery, the shimmer of the unknown. A dash of club soda lifts the mixture with effervescence — the fleeting, ephemeral nature of dreams themselves.

The lavender sprig rests atop the glass like a charm placed on a pillow, a reminder that the boundary between waking and dreaming is thinner than we think.

Raise this glass to the Makers of Dreams — to the visions that guide us, the mysteries that shape us, and the ancient hands that craft the stories we carry into morning.

The House of Riddles

A dark-berry draught of wit and wonder — a sip shaped by puzzles, hidden doors, and the quiet thrill of unlocking what waits in shadow

Ingredients:

- 1 oz bourbon
- 1 oz blackberry liqueur
- 1 oz fresh lemon juice
- 1/2 oz honey syrup
- A dash of bitters
- Garnish: lemon twist

Directions

1. Add bourbon, blackberry liqueur, lemon juice, honey syrup, and bitters to a shaker filled with ice.
2. Shake well until chilled.
3. Strain into a chilled glass.
4. Garnish with a lemon twist.

Deep in the Highlands, where mist curls through the heather like drifting thought, there is said to be a house that reveals itself only to those clever enough — or bold enough — to seek it. They call it the House of Riddles, a place of shifting rooms, whispered puzzles, and doors that open only when the right words are spoken.

The tale tells of a young scholar, hungry for knowledge and restless for meaning. Guided by cryptic clues and the murmured advice of hermits who live at the edge of the world, he finds the hidden house at last. Inside, each room presents a challenge: a riddle carved into stone, a puzzle woven into tapestry, a question posed by a voice that seems to come from the walls themselves.

Some who enter never return.
Some emerge wiser, changed, carrying truths too heavy for ordinary life.
And a rare few reach the final chamber, where the greatest riddle waits — one that reveals not treasure, but understanding, the kind that reshapes the soul.

This cocktail captures the mystery, depth, and quiet exhilaration of that journey — the sweetness of discovery, the sharpness of insight, the shadows that guard the path.

Bourbon forms the drink's strong foundation, the determination required to step into the unknown. Blackberry liqueur adds dark, layered sweetness, the richness of riddles whose answers lie just out of reach. Lemon juice cuts through with bright clarity, the flash of understanding when a puzzle finally yields. Honey syrup softens the edges, the warmth of wisdom earned through perseverance. Bitters add complexity, the reminder that not all answers come easily — nor should they.

The lemon twist curls atop the glass like a question mark carved in gold, a final nod to the riddles that shape the tale.

Raise this glass to the House of Riddles — to curiosity, to courage, and to the truths that wait behind the doors we dare to open.

Where the Forest Opens and the Path Turns
The woods have offered their wonders — soft-footed spirits, green-gold magic, and the shimmering presence of the fae who walk between worlds. But even the deepest forest eventually gives way to open sky. As the trees thin and the moss-soft paths brighten, the enchantment lingers like a final breath of twilight.

Ahead lies a realm shaped not by leaf or loam, but by stone, shadow, and the echoes of ancient power. The next chapter steps into places where the land itself remembers — where ruins whisper, standing stones hum with old energy, and the past rises like mist from the earth.

Follow the path out of the woods.
The stones are waiting.

FAERIE REALMS AND

Kings, queens, and warriors stride through these pages, their tales immortalized in drink. Raise a glass to valor, vengeance, and the victories of old.

CHAPTER 5

ROYALTY, WARRIORS, AND

ANCIENT FEATS

"FAR AN SEAS AN GAISGEACH, BIDH AN SGEUL BEÒ."

"WHERE THE WARRIOR STANDS, THE STORY LIVES."

Where crowns are won, legends are forged, and the echoes of ancient battles still ring across the glens.

From the courts of Highland kings to the storm-lashed shores where warriors carved their names into memory, Scotland's history is a tapestry woven from courage, loyalty, and the relentless pursuit of honor. These are tales of champions and chieftains, of horses swift as wind, of blades that gleamed beneath northern skies, and of the feats that shaped kingdoms.

This chapter gathers cocktails inspired by those heroic traditions — drinks that carry the weight of old alliances, the fire of battle, and the quiet dignity of leaders who bore their burdens with unshakable resolve. Here you'll meet noble steeds, warrior-spirits, royal tricksters, and champions whose deeds echo through time.

Raise your glass to the heroes of old — to the victories that defined them, the trials that tested them, and the stories that refuse to fade.

This opener

Langoureth

A golden, herb-lit draught of sovereignty and resilience — the taste of a queen who held her kingdom together through wisdom, courage, and the quiet fire of conviction.

Ingredients:

- 2 oz Scotch whisky
- 1 oz Drambuie
- 1/2 oz elderflower liqueur
- 1/2 oz fresh lemon juice
- 2 dashes Angostura bitters
- Garnish: rosemary sprig

Directions

1. Fill a cocktail shaker with ice.
2. Add Scotch whisky, Drambuie, elderflower liqueur, lemon juice, and bitters.
3. Shake well until chilled.
4. Strain into a chilled cocktail glass.
5. Garnish with a sprig of rosemary.

In the shadowed courts of sixth-century Scotland, where old gods whispered through the trees and new faiths rose like storm winds, there lived a queen whose story refuses to fade: Langoureth of Strathclyde, the Lost Queen. Her life unfolded in an age of upheaval — kingdoms shifting, alliances fracturing, and the ancient ways standing on the brink of erasure.

Langoureth was no passive figure in this turning world. She was a strategist, a diplomat, a woman whose intelligence shaped the fate of her people. Married to Rhydderch Hael, king of Alt Clut, she navigated a landscape where every decision carried the weight of kingdoms.

Her twin brother, Lailoken — the wild seer believed to be the seed of the Merlin legend — stood at the edge of madness and prophecy, and Langoureth walked the line between political necessity and familial loyalty with unwavering resolve.
Her story is one of quiet power, the kind that does not roar but endures. She held her kingdom together not through brute force, but through insight, intuition, and the ability to see the threads others overlooked.
This cocktail captures the strength, elegance, and layered complexity of Langoureth herself.

Scotch whisky forms the drink's backbone — the rugged heart of the land she ruled. Drambuie adds honeyed depth, the warmth of alliances forged in fire and necessity. Elderflower liqueur brings a floral whisper, the grace and mystique that surrounded her. Lemon juice cuts through with sharp clarity, the challenges she faced and the decisions that demanded precision. Bitters add shadow and depth, the political intrigues that shaped her reign. The rosemary sprig rises from the glass like a queen's standard — evergreen, enduring, and fragrant with memory.

Raise this glass to Langoureth — to the queens history tried to forget, to the women who held kingdoms together, and to the stories that rise again when the world is ready to hear them.

The King of Norway's Brown Horse

A bold, spirited draught of loyalty and legend — the taste of a steed whose strength shaped kingdoms and whose story gallops across centuries.

Ingredients:

- 1 oz Scotch whisky
- 1 oz apple brandy
- 1 oz ginger beer
- 1/2 oz fresh lime juice
- A dash of Angostura bitters
- Garnish: apple slice

Directions

1. Add Scotch whisky, apple brandy, ginger beer, lime juice, and bitters to a shaker filled with ice.
2. Shake well until chilled.
3. Strain into a chilled glass.
4. Garnish with an apple slice.

In the old tales shared across the North Sea, where salt wind carries stories between Scotland and Norway, there is one legend that stands taller than the rest — the tale of the King of Norway's Brown Horse. This is no ordinary steed. In the stories, it is a creature of uncanny strength, unwavering loyalty, and a wisdom that borders on the supernatural. Some say it understood speech. Others say it could sense danger before it came. A few whisper that it was descended from the horses of the gods themselves.

The tale often begins with a young Scottish hero — a prince, a warrior, or a wanderer — who finds himself in the court of the Norwegian king. There he encounters the brown horse, a creature whose presence commands silence. When the hero is tested, betrayed, or sent on an impossible quest, it is the horse who becomes his ally. Together they outrun giants, cross frozen seas, and defy the traps of jealous courtiers. The horse is more than a mount — it is a companion, a guardian, and a symbol of the bond between courage and destiny.

This cocktail captures the strength, nobility, and fierce loyalty of that legendary steed.

Scotch whisky forms the drink's powerful foundation — the rugged heart of the Highlands and the courage of the heroes who rode into danger without hesitation. Apple brandy adds warmth and sweetness, the bond between rider and horse, forged through trust and trial. Ginger beer brings a spirited kick, the speed and fire of hooves pounding across frozen ground. Lime juice cuts through with sharp clarity, the challenges faced along the journey. Bitters add depth and shadow, the weight of ancient oaths and the cost of loyalty.

The apple slice rests atop the glass like a token of the horse's noble lineage — a reminder that even in the fiercest battles, loyalty is a gift that outlasts kings.

Raise this glass to the Brown Horse — to strength that does not falter, to loyalty that does not break, and to the legends that gallop beside us through time.

Lady Odivere

A rose-lit draught of longing and tide-bound magic — the taste of a love shaped by the sea, sealed by moonlight, and carried on the backs of selkies.

Ingredients:

- 1 oz gin
- 1 oz rose liqueur
- 1 oz fresh lemon juice
- 1/2 oz honey syrup
- A dash of rose water
- Garnish: rose petal

Directions

1. Add gin, rose liqueur, lemon juice, honey syrup, and rose water to a shaker filled with ice.
2. Shake well until chilled.
3. Strain into a chilled glass.

In the Orkney Islands, where wind and tide braid themselves into every story, there is a tale whispered in the hush between waves — the story of Lady Odivere, a woman whose life was forever altered by the sea's most mysterious children: the selkies.

Her husband had gone to war, leaving her alone in a stone house overlooking the restless water. One night, as the moon cast a silver road across the waves, a stranger appeared at her door — a man with eyes like deep water and a voice that carried the hush of the tide. She knew him. Or rather, she remembered him, though she could not say how. Their connection was immediate, fierce, and fleeting.

Only later did he reveal the truth: he was a selkie, one of the seal-folk who shed their skins to walk as humans beneath the moon. Their night together had been a moment stolen from two worlds that could never fully meet. His return was not a rekindling, but a farewell — a reminder of a love that lived in memory, not in the waking world.

Lady Odivere's tale is one of longing, loss, and the thin line between the mortal heart and the sea's enchantment. It is a story shaped by tides — advancing, retreating, leaving behind traces of what once was.

This cocktail captures the romance, sorrow, and sea-bound magic of her legend.

Gin forms the drink's clear, bracing foundation — the cold clarity of the northern sea. Rose liqueur adds floral warmth, the beauty and tenderness of Lady Odivere herself. Lemon juice brings bright sharpness, the sting of love that cannot remain. Honey syrup softens the edges, the sweetness of the night they shared. A dash of rose water adds a whisper of the otherworld, the scent of something remembered but unreachable. The rose petal rests atop the glass like a token left on a windowsill — delicate, fleeting, and touched by the sea breeze.

Raise this glass to Lady Odivere — to love that arrives like a tide, to the stories the sea keeps, and to the hearts that learn to let go.

Tam Lim

A deep-crimson draught of courage and transformation — the taste of a love fierce enough to defy enchantment and hold fast through every shape the night can conjure.

Ingredients:

- 1 oz absinthe
- 1 oz apple brandy
- 1 oz pomegranate juice
- 1/2 oz simple syrup
- A dash of bitters
- Garnish: pomegranate seeds

Directions

1. Add absinthe, apple brandy, pomegranate juice, simple syrup, and bitters to a shaker filled with ice.
2. Shake well until chilled.
3. Strain into a chilled glass.
4. Garnish with pomegranate seeds.

In the woods of Carterhaugh, where the trees lean close as if listening, there is a tale older than memory — the story of Tam Lim, the mortal man stolen by the Queen of the Fairies and bound to her will. His fate might have been sealed forever, had it not been for Janet, the bold daughter of the lord of the land.

Janet meets Tam Lim beneath the green canopy, where the air hums with enchantment. Their connection is immediate, undeniable — a spark that cuts through glamour and shadow. But Tam Lim is trapped, held by the Fairy Queen, doomed to be given as a tithe to Hell unless someone loves him fiercely enough to claim him.

He tells Janet the truth:
On Halloween night, when the fae ride out in their wild procession, she must seize him from his horse and hold him tight — no matter what he becomes.

And so she does.

As the Fairy Queen's riders thunder past, Janet pulls Tam Lim from the saddle. The fae magic surges. He transforms in her arms — into a serpent, a burning brand, a snarling beast, a creature of ice and fire. Each time she holds on. Each time she refuses to let him go. Her courage breaks the enchantment. Her love brings him home.

This cocktail captures the danger, devotion, and shape-shifting magic of that night.

Absinthe forms the drink's mystical backbone — the sharp, herbaceous pull of the fairy realm. Apple brandy adds warmth and humanity, the love that anchors Tam Lim to the mortal world. Pomegranate juice brings deep crimson intensity, the blood-bright color of sacrifice and transformation. Simple syrup softens the edges, the tenderness beneath the terror. Bitters add shadow, the cost of defying a queen. The pomegranate seeds gleam like drops of enchanted fire — each one a reminder of the shapes Tam Lim became and the courage Janet held.

Raise this glass to Tam Lim — to love that refuses to yield, to bravery that holds through every transformation, and to the mortal heart that can outmatch faerie power.

The Knights of the Red Shield

A bold, ruby-bright draught of valor and camaraderie — the taste of warriors who rode beneath a crimson banner and carved their legends into the bones of the land.

Ingredients:

- 1 oz rye whiskey
- 1 oz cherry liqueur
- 1 oz fresh lemon juice
- 1/2 oz simple syrup
- A dash of bitters
- Garnish: cherry

Directions

1. Add rye whiskey, cherry liqueur, lemon juice, simple syrup, and bitters to a shaker filled with ice.
2. Shake well until chilled.
3. Strain into a chilled glass.
4. Garnish with a cherry.

In the old tales of Scotland and Eirinn, where battlefields smoldered beneath iron skies, there is a legend of a company of warriors whose courage was so fierce, their shields seemed to burn with their own inner fire. They were known as The Knights of the Red Shield, sworn protectors of the King of Eirinn and defenders of the realm against threats both mortal and monstrous.

Their shields were painted a deep, blood-red — not as a symbol of violence, but of loyalty, sacrifice, and the unbreakable bond between those who stand shoulder to shoulder in the face of danger. When the kingdom was threatened by a dragon whose breath could scorch stone, it was these knights who answered the call. Led by a captain whose resolve was as sharp as his blade, they journeyed across mountains, through shadowed forests, and into the lair of the beast itself.

Their quest was not defined by brute strength alone. It was their unity — their shared purpose, their trust in one another — that carried them through every trial. When they returned victorious, their red shields gleamed in the sunlight like embers of a fire that would never die.

This cocktail captures the strength, honor, and camaraderie of those legendary warriors.

Rye whiskey forms the drink's bold foundation — the grit and determination of the knights. Cherry liqueur adds a deep, ruby sweetness, the color of their shields and the heart of their loyalty. Lemon juice brings sharp clarity, the quick thinking needed in battle. Simple syrup softens the edges, the warmth of fellowship around the campfire. Bitters add depth and shadow, the trials faced and the scars earned. The cherry garnish rests atop the glass like a warrior's seal — bright, proud, and unbroken.

Raise this glass to the Knights of the Red Shield — to courage shared, to loyalty sworn, and to the stories that shine brightest when the world grows dark.

The King and the Cockerel

A bright, golden draught of wit and justice — the taste of a small hero with a sharp tongue, a clever plan, and the courage to stand before a king.

Ingredients:

- 1 oz rye whiskey
- 1 oz apricot brandy
- 1 oz fresh lemon juice
- 1/2 oz honey syrup
- A dash of bitters
- Garnish: apricot slice

Directions

1. Add rye whiskey, apricot brandy, lemon juice, honey syrup, and bitters to a shaker filled with ice.
2. Shake well until chilled.
3. Strain into a chilled glass.
4. Garnish with an apricot slice.

In the lively corners of Scottish folklore, where clever creatures often outwit kings, there is a tale that sparkles with humor and justice — the story of The King and the Cockerel. It begins with a greedy monarch who confiscates a single gold coin from a humble cockerel. The king believes the matter trivial. The cockerel does not.

Determined to reclaim what is his, the cockerel embarks on a journey straight into the heart of the royal court. Along the way, he faces obstacles meant to deter him — locked gates, scheming advisors, traps laid by those who underestimate him. But the cockerel is persistent, sharp-eyed, and utterly unafraid. Each time the king attempts to thwart him, the cockerel finds a way through, using wit where strength would fail.

In the end, it is the cockerel's cleverness, courage, and refusal to yield that win the day. He confronts the king, exposes his greed, and retrieves his gold coin — a small treasure, but a mighty victory.

This cocktail captures the bright spirit, sharp wit, and triumphant sweetness of that tale. Rye whiskey forms the drink's bold foundation — the strength of the underdog who refuses to be dismissed. Apricot brandy adds warm, golden sweetness, the charm and cunning of the cockerel himself. Lemon juice brings sharp clarity, the quick thinking needed to outsmart a king. Honey syrup adds richness, the gold coin reclaimed at last. Bitters introduce

depth, the challenges faced along the way. The apricot slice rests atop the glass like a small, shining reward — a reminder that even the smallest hero can win a mighty victory.

Raise this glass to the King and the Cockerel — to cleverness over cruelty, to justice over greed, and to the bright, feathered courage that refuses to be ignored.

Asipattle and the Stoor Worm

A fiery, sea-bright draught of courage and cunning — the taste of a dreamer who rose from the hearth to slay a monster and claim a kingdom.

Ingredients:

- 1 oz spiced rum
- 1 oz green chartreuse
- 1 oz pineapple juice
- 1/2 oz fresh lime juice
- A dash of bitters
- Garnish: pineapple leaf

Directions

1. Add spiced rum, green chartreuse, pineapple juice, lime juice, and bitters to a shaker filled with ice.
2. Shake well until chilled.
3. Strain into a chilled glass.
4. Garnish with a pineapple leaf.

In the windswept isles of Orkney, where the sea speaks in riddles and the land remembers its heroes, there is a tale of a boy who was never meant to be great — and yet became the savior of a kingdom. His name was Asipattle, the youngest son of a farmer, mocked for his laziness and his habit of daydreaming beside the hearth.

But when the monstrous Stoor Worm, a sea serpent so vast it could poison the sky with its breath, demanded weekly sacrifices of maidens — and when the king's own daughter was chosen — it was Asipattle who stepped forward. Not with sword or shield, but with a plan.

Armed with a smoldering peat and a heart full of fire, he sailed into the belly of the beast. While others had tried and failed, Asipattle crept through the serpent's cavernous insides and set flame to its heart. The Stoor Worm writhed, roared, and died — and with its death, the sea was freed, the princess saved, and the boy who once warmed his toes by the fire became a legend.

This cocktail captures the heat, ingenuity, and sea-bright triumph of that tale.

Spiced rum forms the drink's bold, fiery base — the courage that burns even in the quietest hearts. Green chartreuse adds herbal mystery, the magic that lingers in every heroic act. Pineapple juice brings golden sweetness, the unexpected joy of victory. Lime juice cuts through with sharp wit, the cleverness that turned a peat ember into a weapon. Bitters add depth, the trials faced and the disbelief overcome. The pineapple leaf rises from the glass like the crest of a wave — or the plume of smoke from a monster's final breath.

Raise this glass to Asipattle — to the dreamers who become heroes, to the monsters that fall to fire, and to the stories that remind us that greatness often begins beside the hearth.

The Snake Shirt

A smoky, serpentine draught of enchantment and escape — the taste of a curse coiled tight and the blade that dared to sever it.

Ingredients:

- 1 oz mezcal
- 1 oz green chartreuse
- 1 oz fresh lime juice
- 1/2 oz agave syrup
- A dash of bitters
- Garnish: lime wheel

Directions

1. Add mezcal, green chartreuse, lime juice, agave syrup, and bitters to a shaker filled with ice.
2. Shake well until chilled.
3. Strain into a chilled glass.
4. Garnish with a lime wheel.

In the shadowed corners of Scottish folklore, where jealousy weaves curses and wisdom breaks them, there is a tale of transformation and redemption — the story of The Snake Shirt. It begins with a wicked stepmother, her heart twisted by envy, who conspires with a henwife to destroy her stepson, the prince.

They craft a shirt — beautiful, silken, and deadly. It is no garment, but a beithir, a serpent of legend, disguised in fabric and waiting to strike. When the prince dons it, the serpent coils around his neck, tightening with every breath. The enchantment is cruel, cunning, and nearly fatal.

But the tale does not end in tragedy.

A wise woman and her daughter intervene. They prepare a cauldron of herbs, a potion of ancient knowledge. As the serpent emerges, the daughter lifts a blade and severs the beithir's grip, breaking the curse and freeing the prince. Their courage is quiet but fierce. Their wisdom is the kind passed down in whispers and root bundles. In time, the prince marries the daughter, and the tale becomes one of healing, bravery, and the power of love to undo even the darkest magic.

This cocktail captures the smoke, sharpness, and herbal mystery of that tale.

Mezcal forms the drink's smoky backbone — the breath of the serpent and the danger it carried. Green chartreuse adds herbal complexity, the potion that broke the spell. Lime juice brings bright sharpness, the blade that severed the curse. Agave syrup softens the edges, the sweetness of love and healing. Bitters add depth, the trials endured and the wisdom earned. The lime wheel rests atop the glass like the serpent's coiled form — now harmless, now broken, now remembered.

Raise this glass to the Snake Shirt — to curses undone, to wisdom wielded, and to the brave hands that cut through enchantment.

The Cattle of Pabbay

A warm, island-born draught of hearthlight and sea-magic — the taste of a humble croft, a mystical herd, and the night the ocean called its children home.

Ingredients:

- 1 oz bourbon
- 1 oz honey liqueur
- 1 oz milk
- 1/2 oz vanilla syrup
- A dash of nutmeg
- Garnish: cinnamon stick

Directions

1. Add bourbon, honey liqueur, milk, and vanilla syrup to a shaker filled with ice.
2. Shake well until chilled.
3. Strain into a chilled glass.
4. Garnish with a dash of nutmeg and a cinnamon stick.

On the small island of Pabbay, where the sea presses close and the wind carries old stories, there lived a crofter whose life changed with the gift of a single cow. But this was no ordinary animal. The islanders whispered that she was descended from a sea-bull, a creature of the deep whose strength and spirit flowed through her bloodline.

Under her care, the crofter and his wife prospered. Calves were born strong, milk was plentiful, and the small croft thrived in a way that seemed touched by quiet magic. The cow was gentle, wise-eyed, and loyal — a creature who seemed to understand more than any ordinary beast should.

But prosperity can make people careless.

One day, the crofter decided to sell the old cow, despite his wife's pleas. That night, the cow let out a bellow that echoed across the island — a sound of grief, betrayal, and something older than either of them understood. By morning, every one of her descendants had vanished. They had walked into the sea, returning to the world from which their ancestor had come.

The croft never recovered.
The island remembered.
And the tale became a reminder that gifts from the sea must be honored, not taken for granted.

This cocktail captures the warmth, sweetness, and quiet sorrow of that story.

Bourbon forms the drink's sturdy foundation — the strength of the crofter and the rugged life of the island. Honey liqueur adds golden sweetness, the prosperity the mystical cow brought. Milk honors the heart of the tale, the nourishment that sustained the family. Vanilla syrup brings comforting warmth, the glow of the hearth where the cow once stood. Nutmeg adds a whisper of spice, the unexpected turn of fate.

The cinnamon stick rises from the glass like driftwood washed ashore — a reminder of what the sea gives, and what it takes back.

Raise this glass to the Cattle of Pabbay — to the bond between land and sea, to the creatures who walk between worlds, and to the stories that remind us to cherish what is given.

ROYALTY, WARRIORS, AND

As the echoes of battle fade and the banners of ancient kings settle in the wind, the world of royal courts and heroic deeds begins to soften at the edges. The clang of steel grows distant. The red shields dim to embers. Even the great war-horses lower their heads, their work done for now.

The stories of this chapter leave behind a trail of valor, sacrifice, and hard-won triumph, but the path ahead bends toward a different kind of power — one shaped not by crowns or swords, but by mystery, transformation, and the unseen forces that move beneath the surface of the world.

The land grows quieter.

The air grows stranger.

The familiar laws of kings and warriors give way to older rules — the kind whispered by spirits, woven by fate, and carried on the breath of the sea.

Step forward.

The realm you enter next is shaped not by the strength of arms, but by the deeper magic that binds the living world together.

ROYALTY, WARRIORS, AND

Not all stories end in light. These recipes are drawn from the eerie and the tragic—ghostly whispers, cursed fates, and the chill of the unknown.

CHAPTER 6

DARK WHISPERS AND HAUNTING LEGENDS

"CHAN EIL AN OIDHCHE FALAMH."

"THE NIGHT IS NEVER EMPTY."

Not all stories end in light. Some live in the hush between heartbeats, in the shadow that moves when no one is watching, in the cold breath that slips beneath a door at midnight. These are the tales shaped by restless spirits, cursed fates, and the quiet dread of the unknown — stories that cling to the edges of memory like mist on stone.

In the Highlands and islands, where the land itself seems to listen, people once spoke of omens that walked on two legs, of ghosts bound to unfinished tasks, of creatures who fed on fear or sorrow or longing. These legends were not told to frighten children. They were told because they felt true — because the night has always held more than darkness.

This chapter gathers cocktails inspired by those haunting whispers: the abandoned hut where breath stops without warning, the spectral woman who washes the garments of the doomed, the banshee whose lament threads through the heather, the fox and dog locked in their eternal struggle, the ghostly stable boy who labors long after death.

Raise your glass carefully.

These stories do not simply entertain — they follow.

Death in a Hut

A smoke-dark draught of dread and stillness — the taste of a night where breath falters, shadows listen, and something unseen waits just beyond the threshold.

Ingredients:

- 1 oz mezcal
- 1 oz cherry liqueur
- 1 oz fresh lime juice
- 1/2 oz agave syrup
- A dash of smoked paprika
- Garnish: cherry

Directions

1. Add mezcal, cherry liqueur, lime juice, agave syrup, and smoked paprika to a shaker filled with ice.
2. Shake well until chilled.
3. Strain into a chilled glass.
4. Garnish with a cherry.

Deep in the Highlands, where the wind carries secrets through the heather, there stands the ruin of a hut that locals avoid even in daylight. They call it the Death Hut, though no one agrees on when the name began — only that it was earned.

The story tells of a solitary figure who once lived there, a recluse who sought knowledge in places no mortal should. Some say he bargained with dark forces. Others whisper that he merely listened too closely to the wrong kind of silence. Whatever the truth, the hut became a place where the air felt wrong, where shadows pooled too deeply, where the night pressed in like a held breath.

The tale turns darker when a group of travelers, caught in a storm, sought shelter within its walls. By morning, they were found lifeless — untouched, unmarked, as though sleep had simply refused to let them go. After that, the hut was abandoned to rot, reclaimed by moss and memory, but its legend remained. Even now, those who pass nearby swear they hear soft footsteps inside, or see a faint red glow through the cracks in the boards.

This cocktail captures the smoke, dread, and eerie stillness of that tale.

Mezcal forms the drink's smoky backbone — the scent of something burning long after the fire has died. Cherry liqueur adds a deep, blood-dark sweetness, the echo of tragedy that clings to the hut's walls. Lime juice brings sharp unease, the jolt of fear when the night grows too quiet. Agave syrup softens the edges, the deceptive calm before the storm breaks. Smoked paprika adds a final whisper of heat — the ember of whatever force once lived inside that hut. The cherry garnish rests atop the glass like a warning left at the door.

Raise this glass to Death in a Hut — to the places where silence grows teeth, to the stories that linger long after the fire goes out, and to the shadows that watch from the corners of forgotten rooms.

A Close Tongue

A golden, tight-lipped draught of restraint and quiet wisdom — the taste of a secret kept, a danger avoided, and the power held by those who speak only when they must.

Ingredients:

- 1 oz bourbon
- 1 oz apricot brandy
- 1 oz fresh lemon juice
- 1/2 oz simple syrup
- A dash of bitters
- Garnish: apricot slice

Directions

1. Fill a cocktail shaker with ice.
2. Add bourbon, apricot brandy, lemon juice, simple syrup, and bitters.
3. Shake vigorously until chilled.
4. Strain into a chilled cocktail glass.

In the Orkney Islands, where the wind carries more than weather, there is an old proverb whispered with the weight of experience: A close tongue keeps a safe head. It is a lesson carved from centuries of storms, strangers, and secrets — a reminder that silence can be a shield sharper than any blade.

One tale tells of a mysterious traveler who arrived in a village leading a blue cow, a creature so strange that the villagers could not help but crowd around him with questions. Who was he? Where had he come from? What magic colored the cow's hide? But the traveler answered none of them. He kept his tongue still, his eyes steady, and his secrets close.

In time, the villagers learned that his silence protected him — not only from their suspicions, but from dangers they never saw. His quietness became a kind of armor, a way of moving through the world untouched by gossip, envy, or misunderstanding. The blue cow remained a mystery. So did the man. And both passed through the village unharmed.

This cocktail captures the restraint, subtlety, and quiet strength of that proverb.

Bourbon forms the drink's steady foundation — the backbone of character required to hold one's tongue. Apricot brandy adds gentle sweetness, the pleasant outcomes that follow thoughtful silence. Lemon juice brings bright sharpness, the clarity needed to know when to speak and when to remain still. Simple syrup softens the edges, the grace of choosing peace over conflict. Bitters add depth, the unspoken truths that shape every conversation. The apricot slice rests atop the glass like a sealed letter — closed, deliberate, and full of meaning.

Raise this glass to A Close Tongue — to the wisdom of silence, the strength of restraint, and the stories that unfold only when we choose not to tell them.

The Baobhan Sith

A dark-fruited, smoke-kissed draught of seduction and hunger — the taste of a dance offered freely, a fate sealed quietly, and the beauty that becomes deadly when the night.

Ingredients:

- 1 1/2 oz lightly peated Highland Scotch
- 3/4 oz blackcurrant liqueur
- 1/2 oz rowanberry syrup
- 1/2 oz fresh lemon juice
- 2 dashes Angostura bitters
- Garnish: drizzle of pomegranate molasses + 3 rowanberries on a black spear

Directions

1. Add Scotch, cassis, rowanberry syrup, lemon juice, and bitters to a shaker.
2. Add ice and shake hard until well chilled.
3. Double strain into a chill coupe.
4. Drizzle pomegranate molasses down the inside of the glass.
5. Garnish with three rowanberries on a black spear.

In the mist-heavy glens of the Highlands, where the forest breathes like a living thing, men once whispered of the Baobhan Sith — the green-clad fairy woman whose beauty was a lure and whose hunger was legend. She appeared when the fire burned low, when laughter softened into weariness, when the night felt too gentle to fear.

She asked only for a dance.

But the dance was the snare.

Her hair streamed like smoke. Her eyes shone like starlight on a loch. Her voice drifted soft as heather wind. Yet beneath the charm lay talons sharp enough to tear through flesh, and a thirst that no mortal could satisfy. By dawn, the glen would fall silent again — save for the faint scent of iron drifting through the heather.

This cocktail captures the seduction, danger, and dark sweetness of her legend.

Blackcurrant liqueur forms the drink's deep, seductive heart — the sweetness she uses to draw travelers close. Rowanberry syrup nods to the ancient Highland belief that rowan protects against malevolent spirits, though never strongly enough to save those who accept her dance. Lightly peated Scotch brings the smoke of the glen itself, the land she haunts and the place where many vanished. Lemon juice cuts through with sharp clarity, the moment her beauty breaks and the hunger beneath is revealed. Bitters add depth, the shadow of fate tightening its grip.

The streak of pomegranate molasses glistens like a trail of blood down the inside of the glass, and the rowanberries on a black spear echo the old protections — too little, too late.

Raise this glass to the Baobhan Sith — to beauty sharpened into danger, to dances that end in silence, and to the legends that remind us the forest is never as gentle as it seems.

Fox and Dog

A warm, orchard-bright draught of cunning and loyalty — the taste of a chase through autumn fields, a clash of wits and devotion, and the old dance between trickster and guardian.

Ingredients:

- 1 oz rye whiskey
- 1 oz ginger liqueur
- 1 oz apple cider
- 1/2 oz fresh lemon juice
- A dash of cinnamon
- Garnish: apple slice

Directions

1. Add rye whiskey, ginger liqueur, apple cider, lemon juice, and cinnamon to a shaker filled with ice.
2. Shake well until chilled.
3. Strain into a chilled glass.
4. Garnish with an apple slice.

In the rolling farmlands of Scotland, where orchards glow gold in autumn light, there is a tale told in many variations — the story of the Fox and the Dog, a parable of cleverness and loyalty locked in an eternal tug-of-war.

The fox is the trickster of the fields: quick-witted, sharp-eyed, and always hungry for what isn't his. He slips through hedgerows like a whisper, steals fruit from the orchard, and vanishes before dawn with only pawprints left behind. His mind is a maze of schemes, each more daring than the last.

The dog is his opposite — steadfast, loyal, and unshakably devoted to the farmer he serves. He keeps watch through the night, ears pricked, breath steady, guarding the orchard with a patience the fox can never quite outsmart. Their encounters are a dance: the fox darting in with sly confidence, the dog standing firm with unwavering resolve.

Some versions say the fox eventually outwits the dog. Others insist the dog always prevails. But the heart of the tale lies not in victory, but in the balance between cunning and devotion, each sharpening the other like flint against steel.

This cocktail captures the warmth, spice, and playful tension of that story.

Rye whiskey forms the drink's sturdy backbone — the strength and loyalty of the dog, dependable as a heartbeat. Ginger liqueur adds a sharp, spicy edge, the fox's cleverness flashing like a grin in the dark. Apple cider brings orchard sweetness, the prize both creatures circle around. Lemon juice adds bright tang, the sting of each thwarted attempt. Cinnamon adds warmth and fire, the spark that keeps their rivalry alive. The apple slice garnish rests atop the glass like the fruit at the center of their endless contest.

106

Raise this glass to Fox and Dog — to the chase, the cleverness, the loyalty, and the stories that remind us every rivalry has its own kind of harmony.

Banshee's Whisper

A pale, spectral draught of lineage and lament — the taste of a voice carried on heather wind, a warning wrapped in sorrow, and the quiet power of remembrance.

Ingredients:

- 2 oz Scotch whisky
- 1 oz oleo saccharum
- 1/2 oz elderflower liqueur
- 1/2 oz fresh lime juice
- 2 dashes orange bitters
- Garnish: lime wheel

Directions

1. Fill a shaker with ice.
2. Add Scotch whisky, oleo saccharum, elderflower liqueur, lime juice, and orange bitters.
3. Shake well until chilled.
4. Strain into a chilled coupe glass.
5. Garnish with a lime wheel.

In the shadowed glens of ancient Scotland, where fog clings to stone like memory, there wanders a figure known not for terror, but for truth. The banshee — the wailing woman of legend — is often misunderstood. Her cry is not a scream of malice, but a lament, a thread of sorrow woven through the night for those whose time draws near.

She is a memory keeper, a spirit who walks the boundary between the living and the lost. Her whisper drifts through heather, soft as breath on glass, carrying the weight of lineage, grief, and the stories that refuse to fade. Those who hear her do not encounter fear alone — they encounter belonging, a reminder that they are part of something older than themselves.

This cocktail captures the softness, sorrow, and spectral clarity of her presence. Scotch whisky forms the drink's ancient backbone — smoky, deep, and threaded with the voices of clans long gone. Oleo saccharum adds a shimmering citrus sweetness, like moonlight caught in a bottle. Elderflower liqueur drifts through the glass with ghostly grace, floral and faint as the banshee's touch. Lime juice cuts through with sudden brightness, the sharp moment when her whisper is heard. Orange bitters add emotional depth, the mingling of sorrow and remembrance.

The lime wheel rests atop the glass like a warding circle — a boundary between the living and the remembered.

Raise this glass to the Banshee's Whisper — to the voices that linger, the stories that echo, and the quiet truth that the past is never as distant as it seems.

Cauld Lad of Hilton

A soft, mist-bright draught of labor and longing — the taste of a ghost who works in silence, a kindness that frees, and a presence felt more in breath than in sight.

Ingredients:

- 1 1/2 oz heather-infused gin
- 1/2 oz oat milk
- 1/2 oz honey-barley syrup
- 1/2 oz fresh lemon juice
- 2 dashes lavender bitters
- Garnish: spoon of "vanishin foam"

Directions

1. Add gin, oat milk, honey-barley syrup, lemon juice, and lavender bitters to a shaker.
2. Add ice and shake briskly, you want a soft, cloudy texture.
3. Double strain into a chille coupe or small goblet.
4. Spoon a thin layer of "vanishing foam" over the top.
5. Watch as it slowly collapses, revealing the drink beneath.

In the old stone halls of Hilton Castle, where night settles into the rafters like dust, servants once whispered of a presence that moved through the stables long after the fires burned low. Buckets shifted. Tools clattered softly. Hay rustled as though stirred by unseen hands. And in the morning, the work was done — stalls swept, tack polished, everything in perfect order.

This was the Cauld Lad of Hilton, the ghost of a stable boy wronged in life and restless in death. Some nights he hummed a lonely tune as he worked, a sound that drifted through the beams like a memory trying to take shape. Other nights, when he felt slighted or forgotten, he turned mischievous — untying horses, scattering tools, or whispering just behind a servant's ear.

The folk of Hilton learned his ways.
Leave him a gift — a cloak, a shirt, a token of kindness — and he would vanish forever, freed from his earthly toil. But until then, he lingered between helpfulness and haunting, a presence felt more than seen.

This cocktail captures the gentle eeriness, shifting nature, and quiet yearning of the Cauld Lad.

Heather-infused gin forms the drink's floral backbone — the scent of the moors drifting through an empty stable. Oat milk adds softness, the warmth of the boy's simple tasks. Honey-barley syrup brings rustic sweetness, the taste of the work he performed night after night. Lemon juice adds brightness, the sharp edge of a life cut short. Lavender bitters drift through like a ghost's sigh, floral and fleeting.

And then there is the vanishing foam — a delicate layer that collapses slowly, revealing the drink beneath. It is the Cauld Lad himself: present for a moment, then gone, leaving only the memory of his touch.

Raise this glass to the Cauld Lad of Hilton — to kindness offered, to burdens lifted, and to the spirits who linger not out of malice, but out of longing.

The Washer at the Ford

A pale, fate-marked draught of stillness and omen — the taste of moonlit water, whispered warnings, and the quiet terror of seeing your own story washed clean before it's written.

Ingredients:

- 1 1/2 oz Islay gin
- 3/4 oz white tea syrup
- 1/2 oz elderflower liqueur
- 1/2 oz fresh lemon juice
- 2 drops saline solution (or a tiny
- pinch of sea salt)
- Garnish: thin streak of hibiscus or Rowan reduction

Directions

1. Add gin, white tea syrup, elderflower liqueur, lemon juice, and saline to a shaker.
2. Add ice and shake gently
3. Double strain into a chilled coupe or shallow goblet.
4. Garnish using the reduction, drag a thin streak down the inside of the glass.
5. Serve immediately, while the drink is still pale and clear as ford water.

In the loneliest corners of the Highlands, where paths narrow to ribbons and streams run cold as bone, travelers speak of a figure bent over the water. A woman, gaunt and small, her clothes tattered, her hair long and matted like riverweed. She kneels at the ford, washing garments stained with blood that has not yet been spilled.

She is the Bean Nighe — the Washer at the Ford — a harbinger spirit whose presence foretells death.

Some say she is the ghost of a woman who died in childbirth, doomed to wash the clothes of the doomed until her own kin's line ends. Others claim she is older than memory, a remnant of the Cailleach's brood, bound to the turning of fate itself. She rarely looks up. But when she does, her eyes are pale as winter water, and those who meet her gaze feel the world tilt.

If she washes your garments, your fate is sealed.
If you dare to ask her three questions, she must answer truthfully.
But she will ask three in return — and those who fail to answer vanish into the ford, swallowed by the cold, dark current.

This cocktail captures the clarity, chill, and quiet dread of her legend.

Islay gin forms the drink's bracing backbone — coastal, sharp, touched with peat and sea wind. White tea syrup adds a pale, ghostlike softness, the quiet of a ford at dusk. Elderflower liqueur drifts through with faint floral sweetness, the deceptive gentleness of the

Washer's bowed form. Lemon juice cuts with sudden clarity, the moment you realize the garment she holds is yours. Saline adds the taste of river water, cold and inevitable.

The thin streak of hibiscus or rowan reduction marks the glass like a line of blood washed clean — or washed away.

Raise this glass to the Washer at the Ford — to omens whispered in running water, to the courage of those who ask their three questions, and to the stories that remind us fate is always listening.

DARK WHISPERS AND HAUNTING LEGENDS

When the last whisper fades and the final omen slips back into the dark, the world grows still again. The spirits retreat to their hidden places, the curses loosen their grip, and the night exhales — slow, cold, and relieved. What remains is not fear, but a lingering awareness, a sense that the stories we tell are never just stories. They are warnings, memories, echoes of lives that brushed too close to the veil.

The path ahead softens.
The shadows thin.
The chill that clung to your shoulders begins to lift.

You have walked through haunted glens, crossed fords where fate is washed clean, and listened to voices that do not belong to the living. Now, as the darkness settles behind you, the book turns toward quiet craft, gathered knowledge, and the tools that shape the tales themselves.

Step forward.
The Appendix waits — a lantern held aloft after a long night, offering clarity, structure, and the secrets behind the stories you've tasted.

DARK WHISPERS AND HAUNTING LEGENDS

APPENDIX —

INTRODUCTION

Tools, syrups, and quiet alchemies of the craft

In the Highlands, flavor is a kind of folklore. Honey carries the memory of heathered hillsides. Berries hold the shadows of ancient forests. Herbs whisper of glens where the veil thins and old stories stir. To craft a cocktail is to work with these living elements — to coax out their character, their history, their quiet magic.

This Appendix gathers the foundations of that craft: syrups, infusions, foams, garnishes, and the small rituals that give each drink its voice. These preparations are the hidden architecture beneath the chapters — the subtle work that allows every recipe to speak in its own accent.

Use these formulas as the Seannchaidh once used their lore:
with intention, with curiosity, and with respect for the land that inspired them.

SYRUPS & INFUSIONS

THE HIDDEN ARCHITECTURE
OF FLAVOR

In cocktail craft, syrups and infusions are not merely sweeteners or accents — they are foundations, the underlying structures that give each drink its emotional tone, its narrative color, its sense of place. They are the quiet alchemies that turn raw ingredients into something storied, evocative, and unmistakably yours.

They are also where your manuscript's identity becomes most tangible.

Why Syrups & Infusions Matter
Each preparation is a form of controlled storytelling, a way to bottle the landscape, the season, or the folklore that inspired the drink. A syrup can carry the brightness of a summer glen, the dark fruit of a Highland autumn, or the smoke of a peat fire. An infusion can hold the memory of heather, the sting of rowan, or the ghostly floral lift of elder.

They allow you to:

Build emotional resonance — a syrup can echo a legend's mood

Create sensory continuity — linking chapters through recurring flavors

Anchor folklore in the palate — making myth literally tasteable

Craft signature motifs — heather, rowan, barley, sea-salt, smoke

Control sweetness with intention — not as sugar, but as narrative

These preparations are the grammar of your flavor language.

APPENDIX —
Foundations of Flavor

I. Syrups
Heather Honey Syrup
Rowanberry Syrup
White Tea Syrup
Honey-Barley Syrup
Lavender Syrup
Lavender & Sea Simple Syrup
Smoked Paprika Syrup
Tri-Berry Compote Syrup
Citrus Peel Oleo Saccharum
Gingerbread Syrup
Honey Syrup (Sous Vide)
Green Tea Syrup
Vanilla Syrup
Blackberry Brine Syrup

II. Infusions
Heather-Infused Gin
Blackberry Whisky Infusion
Pine Needle Vodka
Elderflower Rum Infusion
Cinnamon Bourbon
Clove-Orange Rum
Peppercorn Vodka
Cherry-Infused Blended Scotch
Lavender Bitters

III. Foams & Textures
Vanishing Foam (Stabilized)
Heather-Milk Air
Citrus Cloud Foam
Barley-Cream Emulsion
Vanishing Foam (Quick Collapse)

APPENDIX —
Foundations of Flavor

SECTION I — SYRUPS

The Droplet Sigil marks the craft of extraction, sweetness, and transformation

Syrups are the quiet architecture beneath every cocktail — the concentrated expressions of landscape, season, and story. They carry the brightness of a summer glen, the shadowed fruit of autumn, the smoke of peat, the floral lift of heather. They are where raw ingredients become memory made liquid.

Technically, syrups give you control over sweetness, texture, and aromatic layering. They allow you to build emotional tone into a drink with precision: a syrup can soften, sharpen, brighten, or deepen a cocktail's entire structure.

In this section, you'll find the syrups that define the manuscript's flavor language — each one a small act of transformation.

Heather Honey Syrup

SOFT FLORAL SWEETNESS DRAWN FROM HIGHLAND MOORLAND

Ingredients

- 1 cup heather honey
- 1/2 cup warm water
- 1 tsp lemon zest (optional)

Equipment

- Small saucepan
- Fine strainer
- Glass storage bottle

Directions

1. Warm the honey and water together over low heat until fully combined.
2. Add lemon zest if using, then steep for 10 minutes off heat.
3. Strain into a clean bottle and cool completely.

Notes

- Keeps 2–3 weeks refrigerated.
- Adds floral warmth to whisky, gin, and botanical cocktails.
- Used throughout the manuscript in heritage-driven recipes.

Rowanberry Syrup

BRIGHT, PROTECTIVE SWEETNESS DRAWN FROM THE OLD HIGHLAND TREE OF WARDING

Ingredients

- 1 cup fresh or frozen rowanberries
- 1 cup water
- 1 cup sugar
- 1 strip lemon peel

Equipment

- Small saucepan
- Fine strainer
- Glass storage bottle

Directions

1. Combine rowanberries, water, and sugar in a saucepan.
2. Bring to a gentle simmer and cook 10 minutes, stirring occasionally.
3. Add lemon peel and steep off heat for 15 minutes.
4. Strain into a clean bottle and cool completely.

Notes

- Rowanberries are naturally tart; this syrup should finish bright and sharp
- Used in The Baobhan Sith and other Highland-rooted cocktails.
- Keeps 2 weeks refrigerated.

White Tea Syrup

A PALE, DELICATE SWEETNESS WITH THE CLARITY OF STILL WATER

Ingredients

- 2 tbsp loose white tea
- 1 cup hot water (not boiling)
- 1 cup sugar

Equipment

- Heatproof bowl
- Fine strainer
- Glass storage bottle

Directions

1. Steep white tea in hot water (175–185°F) for 4 minutes.
2. Strain, then stir in sugar until dissolved.
3. Cool completely before bottling.

Notes

- Pale, clean, and lightly floral — perfect for Washer at the Ford.
- Avoid over-steeping; bitterness disrupts the syrup's clarity.
- Keeps 1–2 weeks refrigerated.

Honey-Barley Syrup

RUSTIC SWEETNESS WITH THE WARMTH OF CROFT LIFE AND HEARTHLIGHT

Ingredients

- 1/2 cup pearl barley
- 2 cups water
- 1/2 cup honey
- 1/4 cup sugar

Equipment

- Small saucepan
- Fine strainer
- Glass storage bottle

Directions

1. Simmer barley in water for 20 minutes.
2. Strain the barley water back into the pot.
3. Add honey and sugar; warm gently until dissolved.
4. Cool and bottle.

Notes

- Adds grain-soft depth to drinks like Cauld Lad of Hilton.
- Keeps 1 week refrigerated.
- Barley water can be reduced further for a richer syrup.

Lavender Syrup

SOFT FLORAL SWEETNESS WITH A GHOST-SOFT LIFT

Ingredients

- 1 tbsp dried culinary lavender
- 1 cup water
- 1 cup sugar

Equipment

- Small saucepan
- Fine strainer
- Glass storage bottle

Directions

1. Bring water and sugar to a simmer.
2. Remove from heat; add lavender.
3. Steep 10–12 minutes, tasting for balance.
4. Strain and cool completely.

Notes

- Over-steeping creates bitterness; aim for soft floral clarity.
- Excellent in gin-based cocktails and spectral drinks like Banshee's Whisper.
- Keeps 2 weeks refrigerated.

Smoked Paprika Syrup

A DARK, EMBER-WARM SYRUP WITH THE HEAT OF A DYING FIRE

Ingredients

- 1 cup water
- 1 cup sugar
- 1/2 tsp smoked paprika

Equipment

- Small saucepan
- Fine strainer
- Glass storage bottle

Directions

1. Warm water and sugar until dissolved.
2. Add smoked paprika and simmer 2 minutes.
3. Steep off heat for 10 minutes.
4. Strain through a fine mesh or coffee filter.
5. Cool and bottle.

Notes

- Adds smoky depth to mezcal and whisky cocktails.
- Keeps 1–2 weeks refrigerated.

Tri-Berry Compote Syrup

🌢

DEEP, JAM-DARK SWEETNESS DRAWN FROM BRAMBLE FRUIT AND LATE-SUM-MER SHADOW

Ingredients

- 2 cups frozen tri-berry mix (blackberries, raspberries, blueberries)
- 1 cup water
- 3/4 cup sugar
- 1 tbsp lemon juice

Equipment

- Saucepan
- Fine strainer or chinois
- Heatproof spatula
- Glass storage bottle

Directions

1. Combine berries, water, and sugar in a saucepan over medium heat.
2. Simmer 10–12 minutes, stirring occasionally, until the berries collapse and the liquid thickens.
3. Add lemon juice and cook 1 minute more.
4. Strain through a fine mesh strainer, pressing gently to extract the syrup without forcing pulp through.
5. Cool completely before bottling.

Notes

- Produces a rich, jewel-toned syrup ideal for layered desserts and cocktails.
- Used in your tri-berry compote center and as a syrup base for berry-forward drinks.
- Keeps 1–2 weeks refrigerated.
- For a brighter profile, add a strip of orange peel during simmering.

Citrus Peel Oleo Saccharum

BRIGHT, PROTECTIVE SWEETNESS DRAWN FROM THE OLD HIGHLAND TREE OF WARDING

Ingredients

- Peels from 4 lemons (or mixed citrus: lemon, orange, grapefruit)
- 1/2 cup sugar
- Optional: 1 small piece of lemongrass or a few crushed juniper berries

Equipment

- Non-reactive bowl
- Muddler or wooden spoon
- Fine strainer
- Glass jar or bottle

Directions

1. Use a vegetable peeler to remove wide strips of citrus peel, avoiding the bitter white pith.
2. Place peels in a non-reactive bowl and cover with sugar.
3. Muddle gently to bruise the peels and begin releasing oils.
4. Cover and let rest at room temperature for 4–12 hours, stirring occasionally as the sugar liquefies.
5. Once the sugar has fully dissolved into a fragrant syrup, strain into a clean bottle.
6. Store refrigerated.

Notes

- This is the traditional base for punches and citrus-forward cocktails.
- The longer the rest, the deeper the citrus oil extraction.
- Excellent in drinks requiring bright, aromatic lift, including Banshee's Whisper and any cocktail where citrus needs to feel alive.
- Keeps 1–2 weeks refrigerated.

Gingerbread Syrup

WARM, SPICED SWEETNESS WITH HOLIDAY DEPTH AND MOLASSES-LIKE RICHNESS

Ingredients

- 1 cup brown sugar simple syrup
- 3 tbsp chopped fresh ginger
- 2 cinnamon sticks

Equipment

- Sous vide immersion circulator
- Vacuum-seal bag
- Fine strainer
- Storage bottle

Directions

1. Preheat sous vide bath to 152°F.
2. Add all ingredients to a vacuum-seal bag and seal.
3. Submerge for 2 hours.
4. Strain, cool, and bottle.

Notes

- Deep, warming, gingerbread-like profile.
- Keeps 2 weeks refrigerated.

Honey Syrup (Sous Vide)

SMOOTH, FLORAL SWEETNESS WITH PERFECTLY EVEN TEXTURE

Ingredients

- 1 cup honey
- 1 cup filtered water

Equipment

- Sous vide circulator
- Heat-proof jar
- Fine strainer
- Storage bottle

Directions

1. Preheat bath to 140°F.
2. Combine honey and water in jar; seal.
3. Submerge for 45 minutes, swirling once.
4. Cool, strain, and bottle.

Notes

- Ideal for cocktails needing silky sweetness.
- Keeps up to 2 months refrigerated.

Lavender & Sea Salt Syrup

FLORAL SWEETNESS LIFTED BY MINERAL SALINITY — LIKE WIND OFF THE COAST

Ingredients

- 1 cup sugar
- 1 cup filtered water
- 2 tbsp dried lavender buds
- 1/4 tsp flaked sea salt

Equipment

- Sous vide circulator
- Heat-proof jar
- Fine strainer

Directions

1. Preheat bath to 185°F.
2. Combine all ingredients in jar; seal.
3. Sous vide 30 minutes.
4. Cool 30 minutes more, then strain.

Notes

- Adds coastal brightness to gin and vodka cocktails.
- Keeps 1 month refrigerated.

Green Tea Syrup

LIGHTLY TANNIC SWEETNESS WITH CLEAN, GRASSY LIFT

Ingredients

- 1/2 cup sugar
- 1/2 cup honey
- 1 1/2 cups filtered water
- 4 tsp high-grade green tea

Equipment

- Sous vide circulator
- Jar
- Fine strainer

Directions

1. Combine water, sugar, and honey in jar.
2. Sous vide at 158°F for 30 minutes.
3. Add tea and steep 5 minutes off heat.
4. Strain immediately.

Notes

- Perfect for citrus-forward cocktails.
- Keeps 3 weeks refrigerated.

Vanilla Syrup

CREAMY, AROMATIC SWEETNESS WITH WARM DEPTH

Ingredients

- 1 cup sugar
- 1 cup water
- 1 whole vanilla bean, split

Equipment

- Sous vide circulator
- Heat-proof jar.
- Fine strainer

Directions

1. Preheat bath to 149°F.
2. Combine all ingredients in jar; seal.
3. Sous vide 1 hour, swirling occasionally.
4. Cool 20 minutes, strain, and bottle.

Notes

- Excellent in dessert-leaning cocktails.
- Keeps 2 months refrigerated.

Blackberry Brine Syrup

DARK FRUIT SHARPENED BY SEA-SALT SALINITY

Ingredients

- 1 cup blackberries
- 1/2 cup water
- 1/4 cup sugar
- 1 tsp fine sea salt

Equipment

- Saucepan
- Fine strainer
- Glass jar

Directions

1. Simmer all ingredients for 10 minutes.
2. Strain and cool.
3. Store in glass jar

Notes

- Adds tide-kissed depth to berry cocktails.
- Keeps 1–2 weeks refrigerated.

SECTION II — INFUSIONS

The Vessel Sigil marks the craft of steeping, extraction, and spirit-borne storytelling

Infusions are the slow alchemies of the craft — the patient steeping of botanicals, fruits, and spices into a spirit until it carries their character as its own. They are how you bottle the memory of a landscape, the mood of a season, or the essence of a legend.

Technically, infusions give you control over aromatic intensity, flavor depth, and spirit structure. They allow you to shape the emotional tone of a cocktail from the inside out.

These preparations are the backbone of your manuscript's identity — the spirits that carry heather, rowan, pine, elderflower, and smoke into the glass.

Heather-Infused Gin

FLORAL, MOOR-SOFT GIN TOUCHED WITH HIGHLAND WIND

Ingredients

- 1 cup gin (London dry or lightly botanical)
- 2 tbsp dried heather flowers

Equipment

- Glass jar with tight-fitting lid
- Fine strainer
- Funnel
- Storage bottle

Directions

1. Add heather flowers to a clean jar.
2. Pour gin over the flowers and seal.
3. Infuse 24–48 hours, tasting periodically for balance.
4. Strain through a fine mesh and bottle.

Notes

- Floral, slightly herbal, and gently sweet.
- Essential for Cauld Lad of Hilton and other moorland-inspired cocktails.
- Keeps indefinitely at room temperature.

Blackberry Whisky Infusion

DARK, BRAMBLE-RICH WHISKY WITH LATE-SUMMER DEPTH

Ingredients

- 1 cup Scotch or blended whisky
- 1/2 cup fresh or frozen blackberries
- 1 strip lemon peel

Equipment

- Glass jar
- Fine strainer
- Storage bottle

Directions

1. Add blackberries and lemon peel to a jar.
2. Cover with whisky and seal.
3. Infuse 3–5 days, shaking gently once per day.
4. Strain and bottle.

Notes

- Deep berry sweetness with a faint citrus lift.
- Beautiful in autumn cocktails or as a standalone sipper.
- Keeps indefinitely.

Pine Needle Vodka

BRIGHT, PROTECTIVE SWEETNESS DRAWN FROM THE OLD HIGHLAND TREE OF WARDING

Ingredients

- 1 cup vodka
- 1/2 cup fresh pine needles (washed, chopped)

Equipment

- Glass jar
- Fine strainer or coffee filter
- Storage bottle

Directions

1. Add pine needles to a jar.
2. Cover with vodka and seal.
3. Infuse 12–24 hours — this extracts quickly.
4. Strain through a fine mesh or filter and bottle.

Notes

- Bright, resinous, and crisp — like walking through a winter forest.
- Excellent in cold-weather cocktails or paired with citrus.
- Keeps indefinitely.

Elderflower Rum Infusion

SOFT, FAE-TOUCHED SWEETNESS DRIFTING THROUGH WHITE RUM

Ingredients

- 1 cup white rum
- 2 tbsp dried elderflowers

Equipment

- Glass jar
- Fine strainer
- Glass storage bottle

Directions

1. Add elderflowers to a jar.
2. Cover with rum and seal.
3. Infuse 24 hours, tasting for floral intensity.
4. Strain and bottle.

Notes

- Light, floral, and ghost-soft.
- Beautiful in spring cocktails or paired with citrus and honey.
- Keeps indefinitely.

Cinnamon Bourbon

WARM, SPICED BOURBON WITH HEARTH-FIRE COMFORT

Ingredients

- 1 cup bourbon
- 1 cinnamon stick

Equipment

- Glassjar
- Fine strainer
- Glass storage bottle

Directions

1. Add cinnamon stick to a jar.
2. Cover with bourbon and seal.
3. Infuse 2–4 days, tasting daily.
4. Remove cinnamon and bottle.

Notes

- Warm, woody, and comforting — ideal for winter cocktails.
- Over-infusion creates bitterness; taste frequently.
- Keeps indefinitely.

Clove-Orange Rum

DARK, SPICED RUM WITH RITUAL WARMTH AND CITRUS BRIGHTNESS

Ingredients

- 1 cup dark rum
- 3 whole cloves
- 1 strip orange peel

Equipment

- Glass jar
- Fine strainer
- Glass storage bottle

Directions

1. Add cloves and orange peel to a jar.
2. Cover with rum and seal.
3. Infuse 24–48 hours.
4. Strain and bottle.

Notes

- Deep spice balanced by bright citrus oils.
- Excellent in holiday cocktails or warming nightcaps.
- Keeps indefinitely.

Peppercorn Vodka

SHARP, HEATED SPIRIT WITH A CLEAN, MODERN EDGE

Ingredients

- 1 cup vodka
- 1 tsp mixed peppercorns (black, pink, green)

Equipment

- Glass jar
- Fine strainer
- Glass storage bottle

Directions

1. Lightly crush peppercorns and add to a jar.
2. Cover with vodka and seal.
3. Infuse 12–24 hours, tasting for heat level.
4. Strain and bottle.

Notes

- Bright, spicy, and aromatic.
- Excellent in savory cocktails or citrus-forward builds.
- Keeps indefinitely.

Cherry-Infused Blended Scotch

DARK-FRUIT RICHNESS LAYERED OVER A PEATY BACKBONE

Ingredients

- 3 cups blended Scotch
- 1 1/2 cups pitted sweet cherries

Equipment

- Sous vide circulator
- Vacuum-seal bag or jar
- Fine chinois or coffee filter

Directions

1. Preheat bath to 131°F.
2. Combine cherries and Scotch; seal.
3. Submerge for 2 hours, agitating halfway.
4. Chill 1 hour to settle sediment.
5. Decant and filter.

Notes

- Deep, lush, and slightly smoky.
- Best within 6 months.

Lavender Bitters

BRIGHT, FLORAL AROMATICS WITH A BACKBONE OF GENTIAN AND CITRUS

Ingredients

- 1 cup high-proof neutral spirit
- 2 tbsp dried lavender buds
- 1 tbsp gentian root
- 1 tsp dried sweet orange peel
- 5 green cardamom pods, lightly crushed

Equipment

- Mason jar
- Fine strainer
- Dropper bottles

Directions

1. Preheat bath to 122°F.
2. Combine ingredients in jar; seal.
3. Submerge for 2 hours, then cool.
4. Strain and bottle.

Notes

- Floral, bright, and complex.
- Shelf life: 1 year.

SECTION III —

FOAMS & TEXTURES

The Rising Breath Sigil marks the craft of lift, lightness, and ephemeral presence

Foams and textures are the fleeting elements of cocktail craft — the parts that rise, drift, soften, or vanish. They are the breath of a drink, the momentary flourish that changes how a guest experiences aroma, temperature, and first contact.

Technically, they allow you to manipulate mouthfeel, aromatic release, and visual drama. A foam can brighten acidity, soften bitterness, or create a sensory contrast that transforms the entire sip.

In this section, you'll find both stabilized foams and ephemeral airs — each one designed to echo the emotional tone of the cocktails they accompany.

Vanishing Foam (Stabilized)

A SOFT, CLOUD-LIGHT FOAM THAT RISES BRIEFLY, THEN COLLAPSES LIKE A WHISPERED SECRET

Ingredients

- 1/2 cup water
- 1/2 cup sugar
- 1 tsp powdered gelatin
- 1 tbsp lemon juice
- Optional: 1–2 drops floral extract (lavender, elderflower)

Equipment

- Small saucepan
- Hand whisk or immersion blender
- Fine strainer
- Squeeze bottle or spoon

Directions

1. Sprinkle gelatin over cold water and let bloom for 5 minutes.
2. Warm gently until dissolved; add sugar and stir until clear.
3. Add lemon juice and optional floral extract.
4. Whisk or blend until a soft foam forms.
5. Spoon or pipe onto cocktails; allow it to collapse naturally.

Notes

- Designed for drinks like Cauld Lad of Hilton, where the foam's disappearance mirrors the story's vanishing presence.
- Keeps 3–4 days refrigerated; re-whisk before use.
- For a firmer foam, increase gelatin slightly.

Heather-Milk Air

A WHISPER-LIGHT, FLORAL AIR THAT DRIFTS ACROSS THE SURFACE LIKE MOORLAND MIST

Ingredients

- 1/2 cup whole milk or oat milk
- 1 tbsp heather honey
- 1/4 tsp soy lecithin powder

Equipment

- Immersion blender
- Wide, shallow bowl
- Spoon

Directions

1. Warm milk gently and whisk in heather honey until dissolved.
2. Cool completely.
3. Add lecithin and blend at the surface to create a light, airy foam.
4. Spoon only the top layer of bubbles onto the drink.

Notes

- Perfect for cocktails with moorland atmosphere or floral profiles.
- Best used immediately; this is a true "air," not a stabilized foam.
- Works beautifully over gin, whisky, or tea-based drinks.

Citrus Cloud Foam

A BRIGHT, TANGY FOAM WITH THE LIFT OF WIND OVER OPEN WATER

Ingredients

- 1/2 cup fresh lemon or lime juice
- 1/2 cup simple syrup
- 1 egg white (or 1 oz aquafaba)
- Optional: 1 drop orange blossom water

Equipment

- Cocktail shaker
- Fine strainer
- Squeeze bottle

Directions

1. Combine all ingredients in a shaker without ice and dry shake vigorously.
2. Add ice and shake again until thick and frothy.
3. Strain into a squeeze bottle.
4. Pipe a soft cloud of foam onto the cocktail.

Notes

- Ideal for drinks requiring bright, lifted acidity.
- Egg white gives richer texture; aquafaba creates a lighter, vegan option.
- Use within 24 hours.

Barley-Cream Emulsion

A RUSTIC, GRAIN-WARM CREAM WITH THE SOFTNESS OF HEARTH AND CROFT

Ingredients

- 1/2 cup heavy cream
- 2 tbsp honey-barley syrup
- Pinch of sea salt

Equipment

- Small bowl
- Whisk
- Spoon

Directions

1. Combine cream, honey-barley syrup, and salt.
2. Whisk gently until slightly thickened — not whipped, just aerated.
3. Spoon over cocktails as a soft, warm layer.

Notes

- Adds rustic depth to whisky-based drinks.
- Do not over-whisk; the goal is a pourable, velvety texture.
- Keeps 2–3 days refrigerated.

Vanishing Foam (Quick Collapse)

A GHOST-SOFT FOAM THAT DISAPPEARS WITHIN MINUTES

Ingredients

- 1 oz oat milk
- 1 egg white (or 2 tbsp aquafaba)
- Pinch of salt

Equipment

- Cocktail shaker

Directions

1. Shake ingredients until frothy.
2. Spoon onto cocktail.
3. Allow to collapse naturally.

Notes

- Creates a ghost-soft, disappearing effect.
- Best used immediately.

SECTION IV — GARNISHES & RITUAL ELEMENTS

Ingredients

The Blade & Leaf Sigil marks the craft of finishing, intention, and sensory punctuation

Garnishes are not decoration — they are ritual punctuation. They signal the drink's identity, set its emotional tone, and shape the first impression before the glass even touches the line.

Equipment

Technically, garnishes influence aroma, temperature, texture, and visual storytelling. A salted blackberry can evoke a shoreline. A kelp-green twist can suggest a storm-lit sea. These small gestures carry meaning.

This section gathers the manuscript's signature finishing touches — each one a final whisper of story.

Directions

Notes

Blackberry "Tide Mark"

SALT-KISSED BERRY THAT LOOKS LIKE A STONE PULLED FROM THE SURF

Ingredients

- 1 blackberry
- Coarse sea salt

Equipment

- Small dish

Directions

1. Drag blackberry through coarse salt.
2. Rest on rim of glass.

Notes

- Adds visual drama and coastal atmosphere.

Kelp-Green Lemon Twist

GLOSSY, OCEAN-BRIGHT CITRUS RIBBON

Ingredients

- 1 lemon
- Pinch of sea salt

Equipment

- Peeler
- Brush

Directions

1. Peel a thin twist.
2. Brush lightly with saline.
3. Curl tightly.

Notes

- Perfect for sea-themed cocktails.

SECTION V — Tools & Techniques

THE QUIET MECHANICS BEHIND CLARITY, TEXTURE, AND TRANSFORMATION

The Four Sigils together mark the craft behind the craft — the methods that make transformation possible

Behind every syrup, infusion, foam, and garnish lies a set of quiet mechanics: straining, clarifying, steeping, stabilizing, emulsifying. These are the foundational skills that allow you to work with precision and intention.

Technically, this section gives you the framework to execute every preparation in the Appendix with confidence. Atmospherically, it ties the craft back to the manuscript's themes of patience, transformation, and respect for the ingredients.

Here you'll find the essential methods that support the entire book — the tools that make the magic repeatable.

Straining Methods

Fine-Mesh Straining — removes solids while retaining body
Chinois / Cone Strainer — ideal for berry syrups and thick reductions
Cheesecloth / Nut-Milk Bag — best for citrus oils and delicate infusions
Coffee Filter Clarification — ultra-fine polish for spirits and syrups

Clarification Basics

Gravity Clarification — slow, natural settling for infusions
Gelatin Clarification — binds particulates for crystal-clear syrups
Freeze-Thaw Clarification — ideal for fruit-heavy syrups

Infusion Timing Guide

Fast-Extract Botanicals — lavender, citrus peel, heather (12–48 hours)
Medium-Extract Spices — cinnamon, clove, cardamom (1–4 days)
Slow-Extract Fruits — cherries, berries, stone fruit (2–7 days)
Sous Vide Acceleration — reduces time by 70–90%

Syrup Shelf-Life Chart

Simple Syrups — 2–4 weeks
Honey-Based Syrups — 4–8 weeks
Fruit Syrups — 1–2 weeks
Spiced Syrups — 2–4 weeks

Foam Stabilizer Comparison

Egg White — rich, silky, traditional
Aquafaba — vegan, lighter, slightly earthy
Lecithin — airy, ephemeral, ideal for "airs"
Gelatin — stable, long-lasting, dessert-leaning

APPENDIX INDEX (ALPHABETICAL)

EVERY PREPARATION IN THE APPENDIX, ALPHABETIZED FOR QUICK REFERENCE.

APPENDIX CLOSING

THE LAST QUIET BREATH OF THE CRAFT

When the jars are sealed and the last traces of honey, citrus, and heather settle into stillness, the workshop grows quiet again. These preparations — the syrups, the infusions, the foams, the small rituals of garnish and flame — are the unseen hands behind every chapter. They are the quiet mechanics that give each drink its voice, the subtle architecture beneath the stories.

You've now walked through the full grammar of the craft: the sweetness that anchors, the botanicals that whisper, the textures that rise and vanish, the finishing touches that define intention. These are small things, but they carry weight. They turn ingredients into narrative, flavor into folklore, and technique into something close to ritual.

Close this Appendix knowing that every story in this book began here — in the patient work of extraction, steeping, straining, and shaping. And every story you create will begin the same way: with a single drop of something transformed, and the intention to make it meaningful.

The craft is yours now.
Carry it forward with curiosity, with care, and with the quiet confidence of someone who knows the work behind the magic.